BELARUS

Patricia Levy

MARSHALL CAVENDISH
New York • London • Sydney

Reference edition published 1998 by
Marshall Cavendish Corporation
99 White Plains Road
Tarrytown
New York 10591

© Times Editions Pte Ltd 1998

Originated and designed by
Times Books International, an imprint of
Times Editions Pte Ltd

Printed in Singapore

Library of Congress Cataloging-in-Publication Data:

Levy, Patricia, 1951–
    Belarus / Patricia Levy.
       p. cm.—(Cultures of the World)
    Includes bibliographical references and index.
    ISBN 0-7614-0811-8 (lib. bdg.)
    1. Belarus—Juvenile literature. I. Title. II. Series.
DK507.56.L48   1998
947.8—dc21   97–48562
                    CIP
                      AC

INTRODUCTION

 FOR MANY YEARS a republic of the USSR, Belarus suddenly gained independence in 1990 at the end of the Cold War. With independence came all the responsibilities of a sovereign state. Its long history is one of domination by one superpower or another, and the tragedies of terrible purges in Stalin's era, the genocide of World War II, and the nuclear accident at Chernobyl. But Belarusians have emerged with a steadfastness and a vital culture and sense of nationhood that will help them through the years ahead. Its ethnic groups live peacefully together in a socially tolerant society.

Belarus is a land of rolling countryside, dense virgin forest, and abundant wildlife. It stands at the border of eastern and western Europe and has a choice of futures, as part of a new Russian union, as part of the European Union, or as a center between the two. This volume of *Cultures of the World* studies the rich and turbulent history, the vibrant cultural heritage, and the possible future of this newly fledged state.

CONTENTS

A traditional house in the city of Polotsk.

CONTENTS

A war memorial in Belarus. Belarus has been the victim in many wars, including Napoleon's march on Russia in the 1800s and more recently the devastation of World War II.

GEOGRAPHY

BELARUS IS A SMALL LANDLOCKED COUNTRY in northeastern Europe and forms part of the Great Plain of eastern Europe. To the northwest are the newly independent republics of Latvia and Lithuania, to the west is Poland, to the east is the Russian Federation, and to the south is the Ukraine. The country has a total area of 80,200 square miles (207,700 square km), which makes it slightly smaller than Kansas in the United States. The population density is fairly low with only about 100 persons per square mile (39 persons per square km).

The landscape of Belarus is mostly flat and was shaped by glaciers. Large plains are divided by ridges of higher land with a few ranges of low-lying hills. A third of the country is covered in forest, while in the south, the plains turn into marshland. There is an extensive network of rivers and streams throughout Belarus with the Dnieper River being the largest.

Belarus has a continental climate with four seasons and moderate rainfall. Much of the land has been converted to agriculture with flax now one of the principal crops. At the end of summer, Belarusian fields turn into a sea of blue as the flax flowers.

Unfortunately much of the south of the country is uninhabited and unusable since the 1986 nuclear accident at Chernobyl in neighboring Ukraine. The soil is greatly contaminated and it has affected both agriculture and the natural forests and wildlife. Despite this accident and the loss of forested areas, Belarus has a great degree of wildlife compared to other areas in Europe.

Above: **A stork nesting on a telephone pole—part of the diverse wildlife in Belarus.**

Opposite: **A path through the woods in Berezina Nature Reserve.**

An autumn day. These young birches with beautiful white trunks are the first trees to appear as the forest is returned to nature after years of agricultural use.

CLIMATE

Belarus has a continental climate—relatively dry with cold winters, although this is partly moderated by the Atlantic Ocean. It has warm summers and very cold winters, with freezing temperatures and continuous snow cover from December to March.

As one travels north and east the weather becomes increasingly cold and wet. Average temperatures in July and August, the hottest months, are around 65°F (18°C), while temperatures during January and February range from 18°F to 25°F (–8°C to –4°C).

The warm, moist, westerly winds that cross Europe from the Atlantic Ocean have lost most of their moisture by the time they reach Belarus so rainfall is moderate, although slightly higher than much of the rest of eastern Europe. Annual rainfall ranges from 21 to 28 inches (53 cm to 71 cm) with the highest rainfall in the north of the country around the low hills and ridges. Rain is most frequent in the summer months and often delays the crop harvest.

RELIEF

Belarus is part of the Great Plain of eastern Europe, which stretches from the Ural Mountains in Russia to the Carpathians in the south and west. The country is mostly low-lying except for a few high areas of flat-topped hills. These were formed after the last Ice Age (10,000 years ago) when melting and retreating glaciers left behind huge piles of rock and soil that are called moraines.

Like most of the rest of the country, the ridges and hills in Belarus were once covered in forest. They have been cleared however, and converted to agricultural use.

The highest point in the country is Dzerzhinska Mountain in the west, but it only reaches 1,135 feet (346 m). The largest ridge running through the country, northeast to southwest, is the Belarusian Ridge. Another ridge, the Oshmyany Upland, is in the northwest and stretches westward to Vilnius in neighboring Lithuania. Between the ridges lie wide, poorly drained lowlands interspersed with many small lakes. North of the Belarusian Ridge is the Polotsk Lowland, while in the south, the Central Berezina Plain gradually slopes toward marshland.

The Svisloch River, which runs through the capital city of Minsk, is a popular recreation spot.

The Dnieper River is an important source of food for many people, containing over 60 species of fish including carp, catfish, and pike.

RIVERS AND LAKES

The Dnieper River, which for much of its course flows through Belarus, is the fourth largest river in Europe. It is navigable for most of its 1,400 miles (2,253 km) and drains a total of 195,000 square miles (505,050 square km). It is frozen from October to March but becomes very full in the spring after the thaw when it carries meltwater from the surrounding countryside. For Belarusians, the river is an important means of transportation along much of its length, carrying floated timber, coal, ore, and minerals. In northern Belarus, the Dnieper River is joined to the rivers Neman and Western Dvina by canals, and through these rivers Belarus has a link to the Baltic Sea. After flowing through the Ukraine, the Dnieper River reaches the Black Sea, so linking it with the Baltic.

The Pripet is another large river that flows east/southeast to join the Dnieper. Its total length is 500 miles (800 km). It is linked by a canal to the river Western Dvina, forming another valuable route to the Baltic Sea. The Berezina, a smaller river, also joins the Dnieper and is navigable only by small vessels. The Bug River forms part of the border with Poland, while the Western Dvina arises in Russia and flows through Belarus before finally reaching the Baltic Sea. With its many streams and rivers, Belarus has in all about 20,800 waterways with a total length of about 56,000 miles (90,100 km).

There are numerous lakes scattered throughout the lowlands—about 10,800 in total. Lake Naroch, 31 square miles (80 square km), and Lake Osveyskoye, 20 square miles (52 square km) are the two largest.

THE PRIPET MARSHES

This area in southern Belarus was once the largest marshland in Europe. It lies in the basins formed by the rivers Pripet and Dnieper and straddles the Belarus/ Ukraine border. The land is flat with sandy soils and many shallow rivers criss-crossing it. The rivers flood easily and so the land is constantly flooded or waterlogged. The many lakes in the area are constantly becoming choked with marsh vegetation; as they fill with vegetation, more marshland is created. Mixed woodlands of coniferous and deciduous trees grow in this area and the wildlife is particularly diverse. It is usually warm and humid in the marshes.

Wild horses live in the marshland of southern Belarus.

Land reclamation projects have been going on in the area since the late 19th century, draining the marshes and filling in soil to make the land dry and stable. The drained and cleared lands are then converted to agriculture for crops such as flax, potatoes, and rye. The peat is also burned as a source of fuel.

FLORA AND FAUNA

Belarus has a very diverse plant and animal life that has evolved over 10,000 years since the last ice sheets withdrew from Europe. Conifers such as pine and spruce are dominant in the north, while deciduous species, such as oak and hornbeam, are more common in the south. There is an enormous range of bog and marsh plants in the marshland while willow trees grace the river banks.

Voles, otters, beavers, and various types of fowl such as partridge, grouse, and ducks can be found around rivers. Wild pigs, wolves, mink, deer, elk, and pine martens make the forests their home. Belarus has several major nature reserves—the Belovezhskaya Forest on the border with Poland and the Pripet Nature Reserve in the south are two large reserves but several others are also scattered throughout the country.

Many animals including deer are thriving within the national parks in Belarus.

THE WISENT

The European bison, or wisent, which almost became extinct in the 20th century, is closely related to its American cousin, the buffalo. It lives in herds like the buffalo but differs in its habitat, size, and appearance. The bison is smaller with shorter, stout horns and lives in forests rather than on plains. It is an ancient animal and is often the creature depicted in prehistoric wall paintings found all over Europe. By 1945, only a small herd of 40 animals remained in the Polish part of the Belovezhskaya Forest Nature Reserve. This was the entire world population of the bison. A breeding program was carried out successfully by the park and now the numbers of bison have increased to several thousand. Some of these bison have since been sent to other nature reserves in Europe and they have formed the breeding stock for these animals in zoos and parks around the world.

BELOVEZHSKAYA FOREST NATURE RESERVE

This nature reserve lies across the Belarus/Polish border and is the largest surviving area of primeval forest in Europe. About 183,000 acres (74,100 hectares) lie within Belarus. In the 12th century this forest extended from the Baltic Sea to the Bug River and from the Oder to the Dnieper rivers, but over the centuries much of the forest was cut down for building and agriculture and much of its wildlife was hunted. After World War II the remaining forest became a nature reserve.

Belovezhskaya Forest has been one of the world's greatest success stories in nature conservation. It was the last stronghold of the European bison, or wisent. The park carried out a successful breeding program and now several thousand of the animals exist in the park.

The forest has both conifer and deciduous trees—many of these trees are ancient (350 to 600 years old) and have grown to exceptional heights of 150 feet (45 m) or more. Most of the flora is a mixture of both eastern and western European plants. Besides the bison, the forest is home to deer, elk, wolf, boar, and lynx as well as the more common squirrels, hares, foxes, martens, and beavers. Many woodland birds are also present in this nature reserve.

The Belovezhskaya Forest survived because it was the private hunting reserve of those in power for many centuries—from European kings to Soviet dignitaries. It has now been declared a biosphere reserve by UNESCO.

CITIES

Most of the cities and towns in Belarus were seriously damaged during World War II and massive rebuilding took place afterward. Many people migrated to the cities during the Soviet era, raising the urban population from 20% in 1945 to 65% today.

MINSK is the capital and largest city in Belarus with a population of about 1,600,000. It is situated among low-lying hills along the Svisloch River. It has been part of Poland and Lithuania as well as the USSR during its history. It is also the administrative center for the Commonwealth of Independent States (CIS), the alliance of former Soviet republics. Along with being a base for major industries, Minsk is a major cultural center with universities, a conservatory of music, sports schools, and several theaters.

GOMEL, the second largest city in Belarus with a population of 488,000, is a regional capital and administrative center. It is an ancient city with historical records that go back to the 12th century. When Belarus's railways were built in the late 19th century, Gomel became a major railway junction. It is also an important port on the Dnieper River and is a center for the manufacture of phosphate fertilizers, timber products, agricultural machinery, and shoes.

BREST lies on the border with Poland in the southwest of the country. It is one of the busiest border crossings in Europe and has a special cosmopolitan feel with residents of Poland and Belarus frequently crossing the border for shopping and trade expeditions. People come from all over the former Soviet Union to trade and barter for scarce (and sometimes illegal) goods.

Many of the significant towns in Belarus lie along rivers where they have gained prominence because of trade and transportation along the river.

A traditional house in Belarus.

HISTORY

BELARUS HAS ONLY EXISTED as an independent nation since the break-up of the USSR in 1991. But the country now called Belarus has existed in one form or another for many centuries, although ruled by different great powers in succession. The history of Belarus tells also of the history of Poland, Lithuania, Russia, and even Germany, but the unifying link is the sense of nationhood felt by the people of Belarus, their common language and customs, and on many occasions, their common suffering at the hands of invaders.

Belarus has been inhabited since the Old Stone Age, about two million years ago. Toward the end of this period, people lived in caves and had complex tools made of bone or stone, and a primitive religion. Remains of a primitive hunting and gathering society have been found in Belarus, as well as remains of more settled, Neolithic farming communities.

Left: **A war memorial in Vitebsk showing advancing soldiers.**

Opposite: **The ruins of the Brest fortress. This is now part of a memorial to the heroic defense by Soviet troops against the German army during World War II.**

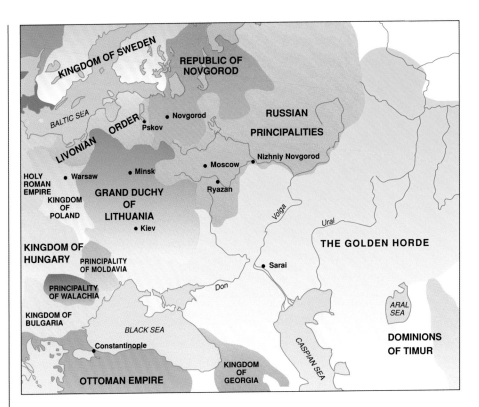

When the Mongols invaded the region in the 13th century, the power of Kievan Rus declined. Countries of the region (including present-day Belarus), however, maintained their independence from the Mongols and were united into the Grand Duchy of Lithuania under Mindaugas.

THE SLAVS

The first Slavs inhabited the region by the 2nd century and are known to have been trading with the Roman empire. By the 6th century the Belarusian Slavs were divided into a number of tribes with a common language—the Derhavici in the south of modern Belarus, the Radzimici in the east, the Kryvici, the largest of the tribes, in the north, and the Drevlyane in the center. By the 8th century the tribes had developed and organized social structures, and the principalities of Polotsk, Pinsk, Slutsk, Minsk, and Turov had been established.

KIEVAN RUS

The Belarus communities came under the power of a powerful Slavic state known as Kievan Rus, based in Kiev (in modern-day Ukraine) in the mid-9th century. A trading empire developed, based on the river systems of the area, creating a "water road" from Constantinople via Kiev to the Baltic Sea.

Many of the present towns in Belarus were established at this time. It is also believed that Christianity came to the region during this period, via Kiev, which first accepted Christianity.

The principalities of Belarus, although under the kingship of Kiev, were mostly self-governing. Each community had a council of representatives from all the villages in the principality. These councils made all decisions and in times of war elected a prince or a leader.

One of the earliest-formed principalities, Polotsk, competed with Kiev for influence over the other Belarusian settlements. In 1067 a powerful Polotsk leader, Prince Useslau the Magician, led an unsuccessful battle against Kievan Rus. Beaten in battle, Useslau the Magician was imprisoned in Kiev but then came to Kiev's aid when the Kievan prince got into difficulties in a war against a southern Ukraine province. Useslau ruled Kiev itself for a few months and then returned to build a stronger, more powerful Polotsk, which ruled over the other principalities of Minsk, Vitebsk, Orsha, and Slutsk. It was Prince Useslau who began the building of the cathedral of Polotsk, the first monumental building to be erected in the territory of Belarus.

During battle Prince Useslau completely destroyed the town of Minsk. This is the first written record that a town of that name ever existed.

USESLAU THE MAGICIAN

There are many legends concerning this ruler of early Belarus who held power from A.D. 1054 to 1101. History tells that he was a magical figure. At his birth, the story goes, he had a mark on his forehead. His mother was told by the wizards to put a band around his head covering the mark. He wore the band, which gave him magical powers, all his life. During the day he was a powerful king and lawgiver but at night he was said to become a wolf. He would race each night from Kiev to Tmutarakan, east of Crimea. In the morning the bells of Polotsk would toll for him to return and direct him to Kiev.

Vytautas ruled the Grand Duchy of Lithuania from 1392 to 1430. During his reign the Grand Duchy reached its largest extent, stretching from the Baltic Sea to the Black Sea.

UNDER THE GRAND DUCHY OF LITHUANIA

Over the next 200 years the power of Polotsk waned and Kiev again dominated the region. But in 1240 Kiev was invaded by Mongols and its power also declined. In the course of the invasion many of the settlements in Belarus were destroyed. The Belarusian population was then absorbed into the expanding Grand Duchy of Lithuania but they retained much of their independence. During this period, the Belarusian language and a sense of common nationality began to develop.

UNION WITH POLAND

In 1386 a union took place between the thrones of Lithuania and Poland through the marriage of Jogaila, the Lithuanian prince, and Queen Jadwiga of Poland. Poland was a Roman Catholic country and part of the settlement was that Lithuania, an Eastern Orthodox country, should adopt Catholicism. This disturbed many of the Lithuanian nobles and peasants, and few of them adopted the new religion.

The union between Poland and Lithuania remained a difficult one with a constant threat of disunity within the heart of Belarus and threats of invasion from the east. In 1392 a cousin of Jogaila, called Vytautas, took over the Belarusian throne, and in an attempt to avoid war, Jogaila gave the princedom of that region to him.

Vytautas became one of the great rulers of the Lithuanian duchy. He rallied the support of other regions, made peace treaties with the Tatars, and later led an army against their conqueror, Emperor

Tamerlane from the Middle East. Under Vytautas, invasions from western Europe by Christian crusaders were also repelled. A union between the armies of Vytautas and Jogaila pushed back the crusaders in a great battle in 1410. Lithuania extended its territories as far as the Baltic Sea in the west and became the most powerful state in eastern Europe. Moscow to the east and Czechoslovakia to the west recognized Lithuania's sovereignty.

Vytautas decided that he preferred an independent Lithuania rather than a union with Poland and in 1429 declared independence from Poland. He died soon afterward, however, and under his son, the union with Poland became strong again.

There followed years of intrigue with neither the citizens of Poland nor those of Lithuania happy and the two great religions, Catholicism and Eastern Orthodoxy, fighting for control of the states. But culture flourished. Belarusian national identity grew within the greater state of Lithuania, and immigrants from many races and religions settled there, including Muslim Tatars, Jews, and Ukrainians. In 1569, Poland and Lithuania joined together to form the Union of Lublin.

CONFLICT BETWEEN CHURCHES

Within the state, conflict between the Roman Catholic church and the Eastern Orthodox church continued, with Protestantism adding to the claims on the people of Belarus. In the 16th century the aristocracy of Belarus was predominantly Polish and Catholic while the peasants remained Eastern Orthodox. In 1595 the treaty of Brest tried to solve the problem by creating a new church called the Uniate Church that was a union of the two. It had the rituals of the Eastern Church with the Roman Catholic pope as head of the church but it solved few problems and just added another claim to the loyalties of the Belarusian people. It failed to flourish.

Above: **For many years, the lot of Russian peasants was not an easy one.**

Opposite: **Catherine II ruled the Russian empire from 1762 to 1796. The miseries of serfdom continued under her, although she introduced reforms in other areas.**

A BATTLEGROUND

The growing state of Russia made repeated attempts to take the region of Belarus from Lithuania in the 1500s. For half a century Belarusian towns experienced battles for control between the armies of Lithuania and Moscow. Thousands of people died during those times. When Ivan the Terrible, prince of Moscow, began his campaign to take Lithuania's neighbor, Belarus again was in the middle and was occupied by troops. In 1568 Polotsk became Russian territory after a truce. In 1576 Russia was driven out. Meanwhile Polotsk had suffered almost complete destruction by fire during the battles.

Other changes also made the lot of the Belarusian people difficult. The Lithuanian Statutes of 1557 set forth property rights on Lithuanian-controlled lands. They reduced the peasants to serfs, unable to leave the land that they worked for the landowners. The little freedom that the peasants had before was totally lost.

The 17th century was also marked by wars between surrounding large powers that used Belarusian towns as their battlefields. Sweden, Moscow, Poland, Denmark, and Cossacks from the Ukraine, one after another, took up battle on Belarusian soil, burning and looting as they went to prevent the enemy from making use of food or supplies. Poland, after gaining control in the Union of Lublin, banned the Belarusian language in official places in 1697.

Belarus continued to be involved in wars not of its own making. Napoleon invaded Russia in 1812 and the escape route of his defeated troops led directly through Belarus.

RUSSIAN RULE

In 1773, under the pretext of coming to the aid of Orthodox citizens, Russia invaded Belarus yet again. The area of Belarus up to the Dnieper River became part of Russian territory. In 1793 a second Russian invasion took the rest of Belarus as well as northern Ukraine.

Russian rule hardly improved the life of the Belarusian peasants. While wars ceased to be fought on Belarusian soil for the first time in 200 years, the language and religion were discouraged and a process of Russification began. The universities in Polotsk and Vilnius were closed. The position of Great Prince of Lithuania was eliminated and the Lithuanian Statutes, the laws which had governed Belarus, were abolished. Belarus was divided into provinces—Minsk, Mogilev, Vilnius, and Vitebsk. Despite Russia's best efforts at Russification, Belarusian culture continued to flourish, even though much of it was outside the borders as 1,500,000 people emigrated from Belarus in search of economic well-being and freedom.

In the 1860s serfdom in the Russian empire was finally abolished. Small-scale industries were set up and in the 1880s railway construction began.

This painting by Marovsky, *Death in the Snow*, depicts the Russian revolution in 1905.

THE RUSSIAN REVOLUTION

In 1863 a widescale rebellion, led by Kastus Kalinouski, against the tsar broke out throughout the Russian empire including Belarus. The rebellion was put down within a year and Kalinouski executed. However, the peasants' desire for greater freedom and the elimination of the class system was not crushed. Building on these beliefs, it was in Minsk, Belarus that the first Marxist party, the Russian Social Democratic Labor Party, was established in 1898. In the first Russian revolution in 1905, Belarusian peasants also joined the uprising against the Russian monarchy. Belarus was granted a little cultural freedom but remained within the Russian empire.

During World War I (1914–18), Belarus again became a battlefield. Vilnius in western Belarus (today in Lithuania), was occupied by German troops. At the end of the war Belarus was allowed to declare its independence and for the first time in history became a completely independent state, although rather smaller in area than modern Belarus.

Its independence was short-lived: in 1919, under the encouragement of Russia, Belarus merged with Lithuania to form Litbel. Then war broke out between Russia and Poland, again fought on Belarusian soil. In 1921, in the Treaty of Riga, Russia ceded large areas of "independent" Belarus to Poland. In 1922 what remained of independent Belarus became one of the signatories of the Union of Soviet Socialist Republics, the USSR. As the Belorussian Soviet Socialist Republic, its temporary independence ended. Western Belarus remained under Polish control.

LIFE IN THE USSR

Although Belarus remained a republic with a certain amount of autonomy, central government was in Moscow. The country's intellectual elite happily threw themselves into the new way of life. For several years the language, culture, and sense of identity in Belarus flourished, while the cities grew and people flocked from the countryside to the towns in search of work.

Joseph Stalin, premier of the USSR from 1941 to 1953, proved to be a ruthless dictator.

But, just as in the rest of the USSR, things quickly degenerated and by the 1930s, under Joseph Stalin's rule, there were purges of intellectuals, hundreds of whom were shot or sent to labor camps in Siberia. Collective farms were created and thousands of farmers sent away from Belarus to camps or even killed. During the period of Stalin's rule it is thought that over a million Belarusians lost their lives. Meanwhile, the four million Belarusians who found themselves under Polish rule fared little better. Belarusian language was prohibited, schools were closed, and political organizations were sought out and eliminated.

WORLD WAR II

At the start of World War II, Stalin signed a non-aggression agreement with Hitler in Germany. They divided eastern Europe between them, with the result that western Belarus (which was in Poland's hands at the time) was returned to the USSR. However, the pact failed and in 1942 German troops, ready to invade the USSR, entered Belarus. German occupation and retreat devastated thousands of ancient buildings, most of the industry, and destroyed the farming system. It is estimated that 2.5 million Belarusian people, around 25% of the population, died during the German occupation, including most of the country's Jewish population.

At the end of the war, western Belarus remained part of the Soviet Union, but the many Poles who had settled there between 1921 and 1942 were forcibly deported back to Poland. Vilnius, handed over to Lithuania at the start of the war, never again became part of Belarus. Large numbers of Russians then settled in Belarus as part of the USSR's program of Russification.

After the war, plans for economic reform were reinstated and Belarus became a model for Soviet economic expansion. Massive growth of towns took place, while rural areas declined. Belarus became one of the most prosperous regions in the Soviet Union. Although it had little in the way of natural resources, great industrial machine factories were established in Belarus to supply the rest of the USSR and the world. Its strategic position, on the border of the USSR, with hundreds of miles of forest, also made it an important military site. Many missile bases were set up there. For the next 40 years Belarus became a region of the USSR, its language giving way to Russian, and its religion banned.

CHERNOBYL

In April 1986 the unthinkable happened. A nuclear reactor at Chernobyl in the Ukraine, on the border with Belarus, exploded and sent vast clouds of radioactive dust, the equivalent of 150 Hiroshima bombs, northward into Belarus. Of the radioactive fallout, 70% hit Belarus. Two and a half million Belarusians were directly affected by the accident and the clouds spread to cover the whole of the country. One fifth of the total landmass of Belarus became a zone of radioactive contamination. The government acted slowly, evacuating thousands of people from the immediate area and building satellite towns around the major cities to rehouse them.

Large areas of land in Belarus remain contaminated. People continue to suffer health problems; children have been particularly affected. Those desperate for land continue to farm contaminated soil and the food, with unsafe levels of radiation, makes its way to other parts of the country.

The nuclear reactor at Chernobyl, three days after the explosion. Large amounts of radioactivity were released into the atmosphere. The reactor core was later encased in a large concrete and steel structure, but there has been concern recently over cracks developing in the wall.

Mikhail Gorbachev introduced widespread reforms to the USSR when he came to power in 1985. He tried to make the government more democratic and initiated reforms in the economy. Eventually the USSR collapsed and split into 15 independent countries.

TOWARD INDEPENDENCE

During the 1980s, great changes took place in the USSR under Mikhail Gorbachev's new policies. They had little effect at first on Belarus, one of the least liberal of the Soviet republics. A demonstration in 1988 was firmly put down but the next year the Belarusian Popular Front was established in Vilnius, Lithuania. They successfully campaigned to have the Belarusian language re-established in schools. The Belarusian Democratic Bloc, a party of all the opposition groups, campaigned for independence. In July 1990 the Supreme Soviet, the parliamentary council, declared independence. It did not become a reality, however, until 1991 when the leaders of the Supreme Soviet were forced to resign and a more moderate chairman, Stanislau Shushkevich, took their place. Communist parties in Belarus were then banned. Later that year the Soviet Union was dissolved.

CONFLICT IN THE NEW COUNTRY

In Belarus, conservative elements remained in control of the Supreme Soviet. Communist political parties regrouped and were registered as official parties once again. A coalition began campaigning for reintegration with Russia. Politics rapidly developed into two groups, those who wanted to retain independence and those who wanted integration. The proposed new constitution contained elements making Belarusian the national language, allowing for private ownership of industry, and several laws concerning human rights. This was opposed by the conservative majority.

With the collapse of the Soviet economy, Belarus has faced serious difficulties. Much of its raw materials and food is imported from other republics, but now those republics want payment in hard currency for their goods or have experienced their own economic collapse. Gas and oil brought in to run factories now have to be paid for and few of the republics can afford to buy Belarus's tractors or trucks. The aftermath of Chernobyl has put a terrible strain on the Belarus health care system and many people are facing unemployment for the first time. Few farm workers from the old collective farms are willing to set up private farms for fear that the old owners will return to claim their land. The issue of language has also become contentious with thousands of people no longer able to speak their native language, Belarusian. The new flag and symbol have been rejected, the old Soviet flag has returned, and Russian is now equal in importance with Belarusian in all schools and public places.

When Belarus first became independent of the USSR, it adopted this new flag, with plain red and white stripes. It has now changed back to the old Soviet flag, which is red and green.

29

GOVERNMENT

THE NATURE OF GOVERNMENT in Belarus has become a major political issue over the last decade. The area of land now known as Belarus has experienced true independence for only a few years. Prior to 1991, some regions or all of Belarus had at various times been part of the USSR, the Russian empire, Germany, Poland, Kievan Rus, or the Grand Duchy of Lithuania.

Above: The flag in Belarus has reverted to a design similar to the one used when Belarus was a Soviet Republic.

Opposite: **Lenin founded the Communist Party in the USSR and was considered one of the great Soviet leaders. Many statues of him were erected in Belarus, as elsewhere in the USSR.**

Prior to the break-up of the USSR, Belarus had been the most Russified of all the Soviet states. Its language is similar to Russian and so was easily assimilated and its government was one of the least liberal in the Soviet Union. Throughout the 1990s, after independence from the USSR, several groups in Belarus have been in conflict over how the state is to be run. The old communists, who have control over the Supreme Soviet and are supported by President Lukashenko, want Belarus to remain a socialist state, with state-owned industry and possible reintegration with Russia. In contrast, many younger people want the economic policies typical of Western countries with free enterprise and individual ownership. They look toward the West for trade and a more liberal way of life. Another large part of the population has grown up in a wealthy Soviet state with full employment and state health care and housing. Since 1991 they have come to associate independence with a lack of jobs, closed factory gates, lines for food, poor health care, and crumbling, unrepaired housing. Other groups, associated with Russian nationalist movements, want reintegration with Russia as a step toward the recreation of the Soviet empire. Many Belarusians abroad talk of civil war looming over the issue of government.

In 1995 an economic union with Russia was agreed on and closer ties are under negotiation.

THE PRESIDENT

The role of president is a new one in Belarus. Alexander Lukashenko was elected president in 1994. He is very much in favor of integration with Russia and has extensive powers to bring that about, as well as the apparent support of a majority of the country. He is increasingly at odds with many other aspects of the government in Belarus, in particular the parliament—the Supreme Soviet.

Lukashenko decided to hold a referendum on November 24, 1996, to strengthen his grip on the country, where a majority of the rural population think romantically of being part of the USSR. The results of this referendum (which many believe corrupted) gave him considerably greater powers and no longer guaranteed the separation of powers in the government. He also disbanded the Supreme Soviet in favor of a bicameral parliament. Although Lukashenko has made several recent economic and military treaties with Russia, they are not being acted on because of Russia's own problems in establishing a free market economy and democracy.

PARLIAMENT

The Supreme Soviet was the parliament in Belarus until 1996. It had 260 members and was elected for a period of five years. According to the constitution it was the most powerful body in the government of Belarus. However, 1995 and 1996 were years of conflict, with the Supreme Soviet challenging the president's decrees and nominees. President Lukashenko's new constitution in 1996 dissolved the Supreme Soviet. A new bicameral system of parliament was adopted against the will of most of the Supreme Soviet deputies. The Supreme Soviet was replaced by a Senate (upper chamber) and a new House of Representatives (lower chamber). The rebelling deputies were excluded from both chambers.

LOCAL GOVERNMENT

Under the constitution, Belarus is divided into tiers: six regions or *voblasti* ("VOH-blahst-EE"); 141 *rayoni* ("ray-ON-ee"), or districts; and below that cities, towns, and villages. The larger cities are also subdivided into *rayoni*. The constitution used to allow deputies to be elected by the citizens of their *voblast* or *rayon* for four-year terms of office. Under the latest turn of events, however, President Lukashenko has changed this aspect of the constitution, disbanding the local councils and appointing regional executives who are nominated by the president rather than elected by the people. Together with the president's right to dissolve the Supreme Soviet and the new weaker structure of the parliament, this does not bode well for the future of democracy in Belarus.

Stanislau Shushkevich was elected chairman of the Supreme Soviet in 1991, in the newly independent Belarus. In 1994, however, he was dismissed after a vote of no confidence.

33

A police guard patrolling the streets of a small village in southern Belarus.

THE JUDICIARY

The independence of the judiciary, like the legislature, is no longer guaranteed by the new constitution put forth by Alexander Lukashenko. The judiciary consists of three courts. The highest is the Constitutional Court. This court can review international treaties, new domestic laws, edicts issued by the president, regulations formulated by the cabinet, aspects of the constitution, and the decisions of the other courts. Its decisions cannot be appealed or taken to a higher court. Another branch of the court system is the Supreme Court. There are also two lower courts, the *voblast-* and *rayon*-level courts. Criminal or civil cases are first heard in the *rayon* courts, which are smaller, district courts. The decision of these courts can be taken for review to the *voblast* court. The *voblast* court's decisions can be appealed in the Supreme Court. However, lower court decisions are rarely overturned.

The third branch of the system of courts is the economic courts. These courts judge cases involving relations between collective farms, for example, or cases against a monopoly. There is a Supreme Economic Court where decisions in these courts can be appealed. A fourth arm of the judicial system is the Procuracy, which is partly a public prosecution service and partly a police investigation department.

FOREIGN AID AND INVESTMENT

Around the world, other countries have been expressing concern about the conflicts within Belarus. In a demonstration in Minsk in 1997, a United States citizen was arrested and then deported for interfering in Belarusian politics. Reprisal expulsions took place in Washington and aid has been cut. Lukashenko's interference in the economy and his return in many ways to communist-type control has resulted in the Western community withdrawing much of its support. When the Ford Motor Company finally decided to go ahead with the opening of a $10 million assembly plant in the mid-1990s, the announcement in Belarus was inflated to an event of national significance—a good indication of the almost desperate efforts of the regime to improve relations with the West.

COMMONWEALTH OF INDEPENDENT STATES

Belarus belongs to what is known as the Commonwealth of Independent States (CIS). This is a loosely structured grouping, founded in December 1991, of the other former Soviet republics, as well as Russia. The capital of the Commonwealth is in Minsk in Belarus. Belarus was among the first countries, along with the Ukraine and Russia, to sign an agreement on December 8, 1991, forming an association between these three former republics. The Commonwealth is intended to coordinate its various members' activities including economic activities, defense, and foreign relations. In 1993, however, it decided to abolish joint defense and instead just coordinate military activities. Belarus, the Ukraine, and Russia also signed an agreement in 1993 on economic integration. Belarus has agreed to free trade with some of the CIS states.

POLITICAL PARTIES

Prior to the liberalization of the USSR, there had been only one political party in Belarus, the Communist Party of Belarus (CPB). It controlled the Supreme Soviet as well as the regional councils. It also supported the coup in Russia in 1991 when there was an attempt to remove Mikhail Gorbachev and restore the old communist system. As a result, the Communist Party of Belarus was seriously discredited in Belarus and the party was banned for a period following that event. It found a new way to function in the state by regrouping under the name Party of Communists of Belarus (PCB). It supports reunification with Russia and a return to communist ways.

Yuri Khadyko, deputy chairman of the Belarusian Popular Front, an opposition party formed in 1989.

There are now several other parties in independent Belarus. A new party, the Belarusian Popular Front (BPF), represents the most active opposition group in Belarus. Its goal is a fully independent, democratic Belarus and it welcomes members of any belief system who share its ideas about independence.

The United Democratic Party (UDP) was formed in 1990. It represents the technical and professional classes and has as its goals democracy, freedom of expression, and a market economy. The Belarusian Social Democratic Party represents a larger range of Belarusians from peasants to intellectuals. It proposes independence, but sees membership in the Commonwealth of Independent States as a possible aspect of independence.

There are many other parties in Belarus, all with fairly small numbers of supporters. There is a peasants' party, the Christian Democratic Union, the Slavic Council, the Ecological Party, and many more. Unfortunately for all these parties, the voters in Belarus seem to have very little interest in any of them. In a poll in 1993 it was found that 60% of Belarusians supported no political party, while only 3.9% supported the Communist Party and 3.8% supported the Belarusian Popular Front. Other parties have even less support.

BELARUS AND ITS NEIGHBORS

Belarus has suffered many invasions and divisions over its history. Many of these changes have come about because of its geopolitical situation. It lies on a flat plain and so any large army wishing to move from east to west or west to east naturally chooses Belarus as the easiest route. Its system of waterways, linking the Baltic Sea with the Black Sea, makes it a strategic target for economic reasons. Its dense forests and position as a barrier between Russia and everything west of it made Belarus a perfect site for arms factories and missile bases while it was part of the USSR.

In modern times Belarus is no longer a stronghold against the West but rather, once again, a convenient staging post on the new trade routes from Russia to its new Western trading partners. Belarus has fairly good relations with its near neighbors, all of whom have owned parts of Belarus at different times, and whose ethnic groups form tiny minorities within Belarus. In the future any of these neighbors could have claims on Belarusian territory. The border with Latvia, in particular, is not yet properly demarcated and all of western Belarus was part of Poland as recently as 50 years ago. Much of Belarus's past was determined not by the will of its people but by geographic considerations and these might determine its future as well.

The national emblem of Belarus, like the flag, has undergone considerable debate in the last few years and its design has been changed several times.

ECONOMY

BELARUS IS A LANDLOCKED COUNTRY and has relatively few natural resources. Newly independent, it found itself heavily dependent on the other former republics of the USSR for many of its economic needs. The USSR had been, to all intents, a single country and so each republic had only a fraction of the industry and resources that it needed to survive alone. Belarus was one of the better-off republics in the USSR.

Even after the break-up of the Soviet Union, Belarus continued to do well, chiefly because it did not immediately undertake the necessary changes for becoming a market economy. However, as the years have passed since independence, the situation has changed. Its traditional trading partners have experienced difficulties, and imports of raw materials have become expensive. In addition, because of the disaster at Chernobyl in 1986, thousands of acres of land are still unusable both for agriculture and for factories.

As part of the USSR, Belarus had been one of the wealthiest states with massive investment taking place after World War II. Belarus was an important part of the defense arm of the Soviet economy with armaments factories, thousands of Soviet troops based on its soil, and nuclear weapons sites around its borders.

Left: **These private flower stands in Grodno were an early sign of a market economy developing in Belarus.**

Opposite: **A woman working at a porcelain factory.**

Milking a cow at a collective farm. Many dairies are located near Minsk.

AGRICULTURE

After World War II Belarus's agriculture was reorganized into a collective farm system as in the rest of the USSR. These farms use the same economies of scale as mass production in factories. Farms were enormous and state-owned with tens of families working on each farm and industrial machinery used for farming. In addition to these state farms, small plots of land were used by individuals to grow vegetables or raise a few hens for home consumption.

Following independence, the decision was made to retain this type of agriculture because so much big machinery was in place that individually owned small farms would not be able to function. Nevertheless, there has been an increase in privately owned small farms from 84 farms in 1990 to 2,730 in 1993.

Agriculture has always been an important part of the economy in Belarus but because of the climate, only hardy crops can be grown. Many of the crops grown are used as animal feed. The soil is only moderately

CHERNOBYL

In 1986, after the disastrous nuclear plant accident at Chernobyl in neighboring Ukraine, radioactivity fanned by wind spread for hundreds of miles and much of southern Belarus was contaminated. Before the disaster, this area was the most fertile in Belarus.

Estimates vary as to the area of land put permanently out of use, but in 1992 it was 642,500 acres (260,200 hectares), 4% of the total agricultural land. Altogether, up to 20% of agricultural land in Belarus has been affected.

Through lack of knowledge, poisoned land unfortunately continued to be used long after the disaster and each time the soil was turned over by plows, more poisonous waste was put into the atmosphere. This continued well into the 1990s. Contaminated crops and animals were sold all over the country so regional markets had to set up stations to check the radioactivity of the meat and vegetables that they sold. Forestry, another vital industry, was even harder hit with about 15% of forestry land becoming unusable. Collecting forest products, such as mushrooms and fruit, as additional sources of food, and hunting for animals also became impossible.

fertile but it has been improved with the use of artificial fertilizers. Some of the swampy lowlands have also been drained to provide more land for fodder crops.

Potatoes are an important source of food with Belarus producing 27% of the output of the former Soviet Union. Buckwheat, which needs less light, is also grown. This is ground into flour or cooked into a kind of porridge. Rye and sugar beets are also widely planted. Smaller amounts of hay, oats, millet, and tobacco are grown, as well as flax and hemp. Most of Belarus's wheat is imported from other former Soviet states, notably Kazakhstan.

Raising animals is another important aspect of agriculture in Belarus. Pigs and chickens are the most widely kept animals, along with cattle for beef. Generally grasses, flax, and fodder are grown in the north alongside cattle, potatoes, and pigs in central Belarus. Hemp farms, cattle, and pasture land predominate in the south.

FOOD PRICES

Food prices in Belarus are carefully set at a level that people can afford. In the first years of independence this was done by fixing the price at which farms could sell their produce. This made things very difficult for farms, which could not pass on increasing costs to customers and were often in danger of losing money on their products. In 1993 price fixing was replaced

by minimum guaranteed prices so that prices reflected the cost of production. In the same year meat prices were allowed to find their own level.

A result of the deliberately low prices in Belarus was that Belarusian food became attractive to neighboring countries and was exported by local people who could make a profit by selling abroad. The term "food tourism" came to be an aspect of the Belarusian economy with foreigners taking a vacation in Belarus in order to buy their groceries at the same time.

Opposite: **An oil refinery in Belarus. The country gets much of its oil from Russia.**

IMPORTING FOOD

By the early 1990s, after the break-up of the Soviet Union, agricultural production was falling rapidly and Belarus had to rely heavily on imports. Since it lacked hard currency, it turned to a barter system and exchanged refrigerators, tractors, and other machinery for food. Matters were made worse by serious flooding in 1993 followed by a drought in 1994. Many crops were lost.

Since food prices are forcibly kept at low levels by the government, it is difficult for the collective farms to make enough profit to reinvest in a higher agricultural output. Those farms that cannot afford tractor repairs or fuel are returning to horse-drawn plows. In recent years crops have become more important than livestock as they bring higher prices.

ENERGY

Belarus produces most of its own power through gas, coal, or oil-fired power stations. It also has nine small hydroelectric power stations. Small amounts of peat from the swamplands in the south are also used as fuel. Belarus is linked through a Soviet grid to several other republics and has recently imported electricity from Russia and Lithuania. There are plans to build nuclear power stations in Belarus but this is rather a thorny issue, especially because of the 1986 Chernobyl disaster. As yet no further extension of the power grid is necessary.

Belarus has suffered a serious fuel crisis since independence. Fuels such as gas and oil that were once freely available suddenly had to be paid for. By 1993 Belarus owed Russia US$450 million. Russia temporarily cut off the supply of fuels as a warning to pay up. Ninety percent of Belarus's oil comes from Russia through the Druzhba (Friendship) pipeline. After several sessions of negotiations and a veiled threat from Russia that new pipelines to the West would be put through Latvia instead of Belarus, an agreement was reached that Russia would supply oil at domestic prices while Belarus would export to Russia anything Russia wanted at favorable prices.

Although much of the industry in Belarus was initially based on heavy machinery, it is now also involved in microelectronics and research and product development.

MANUFACTURING

Before World War II Belarus was largely an agricultural country. The war destroyed most of its farms as well as the industry that had existed. After the war the newly reformed socialist republic rebuilt on an industrial base. In some ways the destruction of the old factories was an advantage since the new factories were able to use newer technology to produce better products at lower prices than their competitors, who were using old prewar machinery. Belarus developed industries concentrated in food processing, shoe manufacture, furniture, linen, textiles, and wood and timber processing.

In the 1970s factories making heavy machinery were introduced. Tractors have been an important export to the other republics and abroad. Other heavy machines produced are trucks, automation machinery, and machine tools. A factory in Gomel, for example, used to produce 90% of all self-propelled fodder harvesters in the USSR. Motorcycles and bicycles, television sets, computers, and microelectronics are also important industries. Belarus also has a large chemical processing industry. In Grodno, Gomel, and Soligorsk, fertilizer plants produce mineral fertilizers from nitrates, phosphates, and potassium salts.

Another kind of industry that developed in Belarus was the manufacture of military equipment. When the USSR broke up, this area of the economy became useless overnight. Since then, attempts to convert the plants to other uses have had little success.

While the infrastructure is in place for a booming manufacturing industry in Belarus, production has fallen in the years since independence.

NATURAL RESOURCES

Belarus has few natural resources; the chief one is forestry. There are about 21,750 acres (8,700 hectares) of forest land. Fir trees predominate in the northern regions of the country along with birch, black alder, and oak. Replanting projects are helping to increase the total forest reserves. Wood is harvested and processed in Belarus, while some is directly exported to other countries in the Commonwealth of Independent States. The wood is used to make furniture and to produce charcoal.

Food items such as bilberries, strawberries, and cranberries are harvested along with mushrooms, medicines, and honey from the forest. Some of these products are exported but most are gathered for the home market. Over 50 types of animals are hunted in the forests for food with about 690 tons of meat produced per year. A tourist industry that arranges hunting trips for visitors has also recently developed.

Peat, harvested from marshland, is another exploitable natural resource, especially abundant in the Pripet Marshes. It is used as fuel in power stations and in domestic fires. There are large deposits of potassium salts and these are exported to numerous countries. There is also a fertilizer processing company within the country. Salt is also mined on a large scale while granite is extracted for use in local building projects. Smaller deposits of oil, coal, natural gas, and iron ore are also mined.

Surveys have revealed deposits of copper, nickel, lead, and several other exploitable metals but these have yet to be mined. Belarus also has small deposits of industrial diamonds which have yet to be exploited.

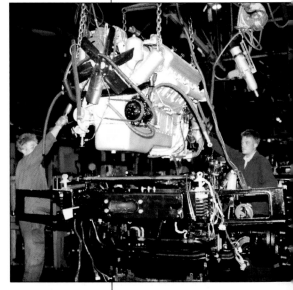

Trucks are produced at this factory. Manufacturing employs 27% of the work force in Belarus.

TRANSPORTATION

Belarus is in a central location in the transportation system of Europe. It is located on a wide, easily navigated plain with European countries to the west, Scandinavian countries to the north, and the countries of the former USSR to the east and south. Belarus also has links to the Pacific Ocean and to Asia.

The rivers in Belarus have always been an important part of the transport system. They provide an international trade link between the Black Sea to the south and the Baltic Sea to the north. Belarus, being in the middle, benefits from all trade up and down these rivers. The Dnieper–Bug Canal, a ship canal, was built to connect the rivers to the Black Sea with those to the Baltic Sea, creating a continuous route. The river routes form three corridors—the Dnieper runs north to south on its way to the Black Sea; the Western Dvina and Neman drain northern and western Belarus and flow toward the Baltic Sea in the north; and the southwest is drained by tributaries of the Bug River which flows to the Baltic Sea as well. In 1995, 1.2 million tons of cargo were shipped on Belarusian waterways.

The railways were built in the late 19th century and form another important link in

the transportation system of Belarus. They carry most of the transported goods in Belarus. There are about 3,500 miles (5,600 km) of railway tracks in the country. In 1995, more than 50 million tons of cargo were carried by rail. Minsk, at the center of the system, is linked to Warsaw in Poland and through that to most other western European countries. It is also linked to Moscow. A north-south line links St. Petersburg in Russia to Kiev in the Ukraine while a northwest-southeast line leads to Lithuania and the Ukraine.

The road system totals about 32,000 miles (51,500 km). Bus routes connect Belarus with several Polish cities. International bus routes, such as the Moscow–Hamburg route, run through Belarus. Minsk, Brest, Vitebsk, Grodno, Gomel, Mogilev, and Bobruisk have electric transportation systems, either buses or streetcars. Minsk has an urban railway.

Belarus has international air agreements with 17 countries. There are seven airports with two at Minsk and others at Gomel, Brest, Vitebsk, Grodno, and Mogilev.

Above: **Tractors being transported across Belarus by train. Belarus was the third largest producer of tractors in the world during the 1980s.**

Opposite: **The railway system is important for transporting goods as well as passengers and connects the capital of Belarus to other major cities in the former USSR.**

BELARUSIANS

THE POPULATION OF BELARUS is around 10.5 million. Of these, the majority (78%) are ethnic Belarusian. Many Russians have settled in Belarus, particularly during periods of Russification by the Russian empire and the USSR and are now about 13% of the population. Other minorities include Poles (4%), Ukrainians (3%), Jews (1%), and a small community of Tatar Muslims. The ethnic make-up of Belarus has undergone radical changes during different points in history. Poles and Jews were once a much larger percentage of the population, and a sizable minority were of German origin.

The birth rate has changed radically in the years since World War II. Immediately following the war there was a baby boom of about 25 per thousand, but by the 1960s the birth rate had slowed to 14 per thousand. As the population has aged, the death rate has increased so that the population figures are currently quite stable or are even declining slightly. The effect of the nuclear disaster at Chernobyl has been to increase the mortality rate of unborn and newborn babies. It is thought that the birth rate will decrease over the next decade or so through fear of birth defects related to the accident. The ratio of men to women in the population is also slightly unusual. Many men died during World War II and during Stalin's rule in the USSR, leaving a disproportionate number of women who are now entering their retirement years.

A majority of people, up to 69%, live in urban areas. There are about 210 major urban areas, with 12 towns of 100,000 inhabitants. Population density is quite low at 100 people per square mile (39 per square km). The average family size is 3.2, while life expectancy is quite low by Western standards—64 years for men and 74 years for women.

Above: **Belarusian children warmly dressed for their walk home from kindergarten.**

Opposite: **A girl and her dog in a park in Minsk.**

BELARUSIANS

Belarusians have occupied this region of the world since at least the 6th century A.D. They are Slavic people whose ancestors arrived in the area from the north. They are thought to be the descendants of three Slavic tribes, the Kryvici ("kree-VEE-chi"), the Derhavici ("der-hav-EE-chi"), and the Radzimici ("rad-zim-EE-chi"), who merged as they settled in the area. Other theories suggest that Belarusians are a mixture of these Slavic tribes and people from the Baltic region. The language spoken in Belarus has some similarity to Baltic languages, which may be a result of this mixture. Among Belarusian academics considerable controversy exists over the origins of Belarusians. But whatever the origins of Belarusians, they have a very strong sense of ethnic identity now.

Some people, especially those who are in favor of union with Russia, say that the early origins do not matter. They look at Belarusians as people who are all from a common Rus stock and who are thus the same as people from Russia.

RUSSIANS

Many of the ethnic Russians in Belarus work in factories.

Russians make up a sizable proportion of the population of Belarus. In many of the newly independent eastern European countries there is considerable ethnic hostility between races that had lived together under communist rule, but this is not the case in Belarus. In the USSR a deliberate policy of Russification meant that Russian families were settled in fairly large numbers throughout the Soviet Union. In Belarus, the Russification policy was very successful with the Belarusian language giving way to Russian quite swiftly in official places.

Russians within Belarus have their own cultural identity and there are several cultural organizations that help maintain Russian customs. There are also magazines aimed solely at Russians in Belarus. Many people have taken up their religion again, which for the Russians is the Russian Orthodox Church. Russian families are spread throughout the urban areas of Belarus and tend to be technical, intellectual, or factory workers rather than farmers.

Like Russians, the Ukrainian minority in Belarus merges into the community, using Russian as their language of communication and practicing Orthodox Christianity.

POLES

Poles make up about 4% of the population. They live chiefly in the western region of the country, close to the Polish border. Once a much larger proportion of the population in farming communities and small businesses, they were forcibly deported under Stalin's rule. They have maintained strong ties to Poland and their customs and dress as well as their appearance distinguish them from Belarusians or Russians. Their religion is Roman Catholicism and they conduct services in Polish.

JEWS

Although they make up only 1% of the population of Belarus now, Jews have had a significant effect on the life and culture of the country. Before World War II they dominated Belarusian business life, forming more than 50% of the population in urban areas and 10% of the country as a whole. About 2.2 million Jews were murdered during World War II and another 700,000 Jews "disappeared" under Stalin. Under Soviet rule many Jews emigrated, and since independence, large numbers have left for Israel.

The current population figures for Jews are probably wildly inaccurate for several reasons.

One is that all citizens of the USSR had to carry internal passports stating their ethnic identity. Many Jews registered as ethnic Belarusians to avoid discrimination. In modern times many young people are learning for the first time that they are in fact Jewish now that their parents feel safe enough to tell them about their origins. Many of them are rediscovering their cultural and religious origins and there is a religious revival among Jews in Belarus. Others are using their Jewish roots as a way to leave for Israel where they can easily become citizens and where they hope they will have some better economic opportunities.

OTHERS

About 1% of the population of Belarus are people from former Soviet states who were resettled in Belarus, such as Lithuanians and Latvians. One small but culturally discrete group is the Tatars, a Muslim group, who were also encouraged to settle in small groups around the USSR. There is also a small population of Ukrainians.

Above: **There is a small number of Gypsies in Belarus. This family is having lunch on the trunk of their car.**

Opposite: **Menachem Begin (1913–92) was born in Brest. He escaped from Belarus when the Germans invaded in World War II. He was very active in the formation of the Israel state and was prime minister of Israel from 1977 to 1983.**

NATIONAL DRESS

The national dress is not reserved only for special folk festivals in Belarus. Country people still wear traditional dress on fair days and during traditional festivals and other kinds of celebrations. The most distinctive feature of Belarusian traditional dress, for both men and women, is the beautifully embroidered linen shirts and blouses. Men's shirts are often embroidered around the collar, sleeves, and across the chest. The pattern of the embroidery differs from region to region and someone with a little knowledge can tell where a person comes from by the embroidery on his or her clothes. There were once at least a hundred different styles of embroidery in Belarus. In some regions the embroidery is all in red and white, while in others many colors are used.

Both shirts and blouses are long-sleeved. A sleeveless jacket is worn over them; this is usually green or blue and laces up in front. The fancier jackets are embroidered in silver or gold thread, or have silk ribbons sewn onto them.

WOMEN'S JEWELRY AND HAIR STYLES

Traditional jewelry for women uses amber beads or perhaps red coral or silver. The amber is worn in three strands, silver in one strand, and coral in as many as ten, probably a reflection of the price.

In the northwest of the country silverwork is a well-known craft and typical jewelry has tiny beads mixed with larger, bubblelike spheres. Clasps are often used to fasten the bodice and can be crafted of silver or bronze.

The typical traditional hairstyle for women was two long braids left hanging or wound elaborately around the head. In the summer, flowers would be added. For special occasions, especially weddings, women wore a linen hat shaped like a crown. These were highly ornate with metal threads sewn into them. More commonly worn was a headshawl with an embroidered section at the front and the ends wound around the face or neck.

Winter skirts are usually woven from wool. Their Belarusian name is *andraki* ("and-RARK-ee"). They are often patterned with woven lozenges or stripes in the fabric and are calf- or floor-length. At the waist, women wear a sash knotted at the back with the ends hanging to the hem of the skirt. Over the skirt an apron of fine linen is worn. A pattern of horizontal bars of stars or flowers is woven into this.

Men's clothes are similar, with embroidered shirts, linen trousers for summer and wool for winter, and sleeveless jackets. Outdoor clothes for both men and women consist of sheepskin jackets embroidered with wool, felt boots, and hooded garments made of thick cloth. The outer coats are usually white with red embroidery for the Gomel region and deep blue cord for the Bykhov region, while for other regions green cord or black leather is common. Men's waist bands are woven with herringbone or diamond designs in the weave. They are tied at the side and the tails hang to the knee. Men's hats are cone-shaped and called *magerki* ("mag-ERK-ee"). They are usually made of felt but some are made of sheepskin.

SOME FAMOUS BELARUSIANS

Many famous people came originally from Belarus. Many Jews, in particular, have left Belarus for the United States or Israel to start new lives. Marc Chagall, the artist, lived in Belarus until his early adulthood. He was born in Vitebsk when it was a part of Russia. When it became part of the Belorussian Soviet Socialist Republic, Chagall enthusiastically took a leading role in the new regime, but he got disillusioned and left the country soon after, never to return. Menachem Begin, a former prime minister of Israel, was also born in Belarus. During World War II he lost his family but managed to escape to Israel.

A famous American composer, Irving Berlin, was born in 1888 in Mogilev but moved with his family to the United States. He wrote many popular songs including "White Christmas," "Puttin' on the Ritz," and "There's no Business Like Show Business," as well as the scores for musicals such as *Easter Parade* and *White Christmas*. Sir Isaac Schoenberg is very important for the history of television. He invented the world's first high definition television system. He was born in Pinsk in 1880 and lived in the USSR until 1914 when he emigrated to Britain. He set up Russia's first radio stations.

Within Belarus, well known people include ancient scholars such as Saint Efrasinnia of Polotsk, a 12th century religious leader, Frances Skaryna, who was the first person to print the Bible in Belarusian, and Symon Budny, a 16th century writer in the Belarusian language. Symon Budny had radical ideas for his time. He strongly criticized the church clergy who made no effort to explain religion to the common people. He was a priest in the Calvinist church for a while, but was ejected from the community after publishing his most important work, which was concerned with religion, politics, and the rights of the individual.

Belarus today has several famous sports personalities. Vitaly Scherbo, a six-time gold medallist in gymnastics, represented Belarus in the Atlanta Olympics in 1996. The gymnast Olga Korbut grew up in Belarus and represented the USSR in the Olympics in 1972 and 1976. She won three gold medals and a silver in the 1972 Olympics where she became the first person to do a backward somersault on the uneven parallel bars.

Above: Vitaly Scherbo is a famous Belarusian gymnast.

Opposite: Irving Berlin (1888–1989) immigrated with his family to New York in 1893. He became an important composer in the United States and wrote the score for many famous musicals both on Broadway and in movies.

LIFESTYLE

OVER THE PAST DECADE OR SO, the lives of the people of Belarus have undergone the most radical changes imaginable. They have taken part in the dismantling of one of the most powerful empires in history; they have suffered the economic upheaval resulting from the changeover from a managed, state-run economy to a free market; they have seen the sureties of their lives such as guaranteed employment for life and free health care gradually give way to food shortages, closed factories, and rationing; and, worst of all, they have lived, and continue to live with, the consequences of Chernobyl, the worst nuclear accident ever to happen.

Amid these upheavals, the people of Belarus are getting on with their lives and making decisions about their country's future that may either lead them back to union with Russia or to a future of independence and closer ties with the West.

Left: **Outside the cities, people live in their own single-story homes.**

Opposite: **A young accordionist making a living in Minsk.**

LIFE IN THE CITIES

Belarusians live their lives in the same way as millions of other Europeans. The majority of people live in cities and travel to work each day in modern, mass transportation systems.

Minsk, the capital, is a modern city that was almost completely rebuilt after the destruction of World War II. The city center has long, wide, straight roads lined with comparatively small apartment and office buildings. Most citizens live in the suburbs in huge, multistory housing developments. Amenities such as nursery schools, shopping centers, and movie theaters are close by and buildings are surrounded by trees and parks rather than major highways. These 75 acre (30 hectare) developments have names such as Vostok 1 and Vostok 2, and house anywhere from 15,000 to 50,000 residents.

Between 1971 and 1975, 47 million square feet (4 million square meters) of housing was built. Most housing is owned by the government and rents have been kept artificially low so that on average housing costs are no more than 7% of the average family budget. Some people have built their own homes with government subsidies.

Many of the people in Minsk work in heavy industry and build tractors, television sets,

OTHER CITIES IN BELARUS

While Minsk is a thriving, modern industrial and cultural center, other cities in Belarus have a different atmosphere and cultural and social life.

After Minsk, Brest is the most vibrant city in Belarus. It is near the border with Poland, and for many years was actually part of Poland. Brest has all the atmosphere of a border town with both Poles and Belarusians making use of the border crossing for quick shopping trips. A black market of scarce goods is regularly held in Brest.

Grodno, in the west of the country, is very close to Lithuania and, having suffered less in World War II, has many more historical buildings than Minsk.

Vitebsk, in the north of the country, also has a historic atmosphere. It is an ancient town that spent some of its history as part of Russia.

Polotsk has a different atmosphere altogether. Compared with the industrial might of Minsk and the cultural heritage of Vitebsk, it seems a sleepy river town. Yet it was once the most important city in Belarus and at various times has been part of Lithuania, Poland, and Russia. Its many historical buildings have survived because the town has seen less industrial development than other places.

motorcycles, electrical items, and other factory goods. Like the city buildings, many of the factories were also built after World War II. Cars are a luxury item for individuals to own, so most people travel to and from work on public transportation, either by streetcar or bus.

At home most people own a television, a refrigerator, and perhaps a videocassette recorder. Homes are small but quite modern with sound and heat insulation. Most people live in small family units. Married couples sometimes live with their parents while waiting for their own apartment. Housing has become a problem since the Chernobyl disaster when thousands of people had to be resettled around the cities in specially built housing. As a result, people sometimes have to wait for an apartment to become available.

Opposite: **Terminal square in Minsk, the capital city of Belarus.**

LIFE IN THE COUNTRY

In the country, life is a little slower and more relaxed than in the fast-paced cities. The small family-owned farms that once dominated the countryside of Belarus have long given way to collective farms, and people live in small village communities in separate houses.

While newer houses are made from brick or prefabricated pieces, there are still many traditional wooden houses. These were once built by the whole village community as they were needed, all in the same style. A wooden shingle or thatched roof covered a one-story building of two rooms. Built onto it was a lean-to, used as a spare bedroom, storage room, or a place to sleep in the heat of summer.

Inside the country house, furniture consists of simple wooden planks placed around the walls. These often serve as beds with a simple mattress of feathers or straw thrown on. In traditional houses, embroidered linen cloths decorate the walls. A simple staircase leads up to the attic where cured food is stored. Older houses also have a cellar.

THE DECLINE OF RURAL COMMUNITIES

As the gradual industrialization of Belarus has brought about migrations to the cities, village life has declined to the point where in many places entire villages stand deserted. This has had a negative effect on the survival of the culture of Belarus because it is the rural areas where age-old traditions survive.

As villages grow less populated, many traditions have disappeared. Added to the gradual migration of rural families to the cities, people in the country are also having smaller families. Where once the typical rural family consisted of 3.3 members it is now only three, lower than the national average.

Rural houses often have a garden with fruit trees, a shed for gardening tools, and a vegetable plot. In addition to vegetables, a family will often have hens and perhaps goats or a pig being fattened. When farms were smaller, the sheds would have held the plow, horses, space for curing and smoking food, and a threshing room. Now the main business of the farm is carried out in huge factory-like buildings where the food is partly processed before being sent on to markets or factories.

In the villages, schools are small and rural in nature. They often include a small farm, fish pond, or a museum.

The communal bathhouse is another feature of rural life. Called a *banya* ("BAN-yah"), the bathhouse may be owned by a single family or shared by neighbors. It is much like a sauna, built of wood and standing in the open, near a lake or river. Inside is a wood-heated stove. Water scented with mint leaves or juice from birch trees is thrown onto the hot stove, creating a fragrant, steam-filled atmosphere. A good steaming in the sauna is followed by a roll in the snow or a quick dip into the river or lake.

Houses in the same village may have similar patterns on the gables of their roofs. In one area, for example, all the gables have a carving of the sun surrounded by foliage.

WOMEN AND THE FAMILY

Nuclear families are the norm in Belarus, and a high proportion of people choose marriage over cohabitation or living alone. Children are considered important to the family, if not the single most important reason for marrying. Women have had economic equality in Belarus for many years; in most cases this means that a much higher burden falls on the women's shoulders, as they take on responsibility for both their children and their job. For the majority of families, both parents working is essential for survival rather than a career choice.

Women usually work in low-paid industries, so women's wages in general are about one-third lower than men's. As the economy slows down, women's lives have grown harder, with less leisure time or opportunities for education, and less cash for buying or repairing domestic appliances to make their daily chores easier. Some Belarusian women see the equality that they gained under the Soviet system, when women were urged to work, as a backward step.

EDUCATION

Education is compulsory in Belarus between the ages of 7 and 17. Pre-school education is subsidized by the state and up to 60% of children attend nursery school. School costs and textbooks are paid for by the state. Teaching is largely in Russian, although Belarusian has been reinstated.

At the age of 15, students can continue with their academic studies or change to a vocational or specialist school of some kind. Children with particular aptitudes can attend schools dedicated to music, foreign languages, math, science, or sports. The vocational schools include schools of car maintenance, building, teacher training, machine building, radio technology, and many others. Sports schools are very important in Belarus with 64 in Minsk alone. There are also specialist schools for athletics, horse-riding, fencing, and gymnastics.

Of the 33 tertiary institutions in Belarus, 14 are in the capital, Minsk. Minsk has two universities, a medical school, and institutes of technology, agriculture, languages, theater, and fine arts among others. Here, an art class is hard at work outside the Cathedral of the Holy Ghost in Minsk.

MARRIAGE

In modern-day Belarus, wedding celebrations are similar to those in many Western countries. However, some rural villages still observe a few traditional customs. For instance, marriages in villages are sometimes arranged by the parents, though only with the agreement of their children. In small villages, the bride-to-be will travel around the village to invite everyone to the wedding, but in towns and cities, wedding invitations are mailed. In rural areas people also still prepare a special bread for the wedding day; this is large, round, and ornately decorated with pine cones.

For all weddings now, the couple must marry at the local registry office, but many couples also take part in a ceremony at their church or synagogue. The bride wears a white or pink dress, though in some areas the dress is traditionally blue. She wears flowers in her hair and is often attended by bridesmaids. The groom and his party wear white and blue flowers, while the bride and her party wear white and pink flowers. The couple is usually formally engaged first, with the approval of their parents and the exchanging of rings. After the registry office formalities, the wedding party goes on to the church for the religious service.

After the couple takes their marriage vows, everyone is invited to the bride's home or to a restaurant for a celebratory meal. The bride and groom cut the wedding cake at this event. The guests bring gifts of cash, embroidery, or some useful object for the house.

Many weddings in the cities and towns take two days: one day for the official wedding at the registry office and another for the religious service and party.

CHILDREN

When a baby is about two months old, Christian Belarusians hold a christening ceremony in which godparents are chosen for the baby, guests bring gifts, and there is a party at the family home.

Traditionally, the new grandmother was driven around to friends to bring the good news. Men fired their guns into the air and the grandmother served the guests *babina kasha* ("bah-BEE-nah KAH-sha"), the traditional old lady's porridge.

LIFE AFTER CHERNOBYL

It is easy, a decade after the nuclear accident at Chernobyl, to sweep it aside as if it was now all over and done with, but for many people this is not the case. Thousands of people are still living within the contaminated zone in southern Belarus, which will continue to be a health hazard in the foreseeable future.

Immediately after the accident, thousands of people were evacuated from the area and new housing developments were built to accommodate them. But this was at a time when the economy was failing and industries could not provide sufficient jobs. Many therefore chose to return to their contaminated land while people from other areas migrated there to take up the empty houses, farm the land, and gather fruits and berries from the forest.

The Belarusian government has limited funds to help the residents of the contaminated zone buy fresh produce or get the medical and social help that they need. Organizations from around the world have stepped in to help these people by donating medical equipment, establishing medical centers for monitoring health in the region, and providing trips abroad for the local children.

A somber gathering of people in Minsk to commemorate the victims of Chernobyl.

The chief danger for people in these contaminated zones is the soil rather than the air. Radiation is transferred from the soil to plants and, if the soil is turned, into the air. In the years following the explosion this was not understood so farming in the region continued and crops that contained unsafe levels of radiation were sold all over the country. Some collective farms continued to produce food even after the soil had been declared unsafe and food production banned. Forest products such as mushrooms and berries are particularly susceptible to contamination. As they are harvested and sold in the markets, they spread the contamination around the country. Dust storms and the wheels of vehicles entering the area also carry the contamination around Belarus.

Life is harder for people in the contaminated zone because of a lack of teachers willing to move there and a shortage of workers to provide basic services such as water, gas, and sewage. There is a high rate of depression and alcoholism among adults living there.

This priest makes regular visits to help people who refuse to leave their contaminated homes in the Chernobyl area.

HEALTH

Like education, health care is free in Belarus, although it has become severely strained because of increased health problems after the nuclear accident at Chernobyl. There has been a massive rise in the number of child thyroid cancers, a long-term illness. At least 2,000 children currently suffer from this disorder, which needs continuous observation and treatment even after surgery. One estimate suggests that the number of cases could rise to 10,000 with a possible 1,000 deaths. There has also been a general decline in the health of children. At present the infant mortality rate in Belarus is twice that of the United States. HIV has also become a serious problem in Belarus partly due to a home-grown drug that is used with unsterilized needles.

RELIGION

FOR 70 YEARS OR SO, from the Russian revolution in 1917 to independence in the late 1980s, Belarus was officially an atheist country. All religions were severely restricted and many leading church figures fled abroad to set up communities in Britain, the United States, and Europe. Since independence, however, there has been an enormous revival in religious belief and worship as young people seek their religious roots and try to find a spiritual aspect to their lives that they felt was lacking under a communist regime. But religion and politics are inextricably mixed. The religious groups that have undergone a revival in Belarus have a political as well as a religious agenda for the country.

Above: **In a cathedral in Minsk, candles are lit during the service.**

Opposite: **This church near Grodno is full of worshipers during the Peter and Paul festival.**

There are two main branches of Christianity in Belarus: the Orthodox Church and the Roman Catholic Church. There are some Protestant Christian groups and also small Jewish and Muslim communities. Large numbers of people remain atheist.

EARLY RELIGIONS

The earliest religions in Belarus were non-Christian. Before A.D. 990, Slavic tribes called the Kryvici worshiped their sun god Yaryla. Their religion was Druidic in nature and revolved around the seasons. Rituals in spring encouraged the beginning of the new season, while in April and October the dead were commemorated with food and drinks brought to the graves. Kaliady, a celebration of the winter solstice, is still celebrated today in Belarus.

Religious artifacts from the early period include stone obelisks used for sacrifices and figures carved out of stone.

THE ORTHODOX CHURCH

Christianity came to Belarus in A.D. 990 in the form of Eastern Orthodoxy. This form of Christianity historically accepts church leadership from Constantinople rather than the Pope in Rome. It differs from the Catholic Church in some of its beliefs and rituals. Several religious figures, including Saint Efrasinnia of Polotsk and Simeon Polotsky, were very influential in the Church's history.

Eastern Orthodoxy became the official religion of Greater Lithuania when it was embraced by the rulers of Kievan Rus. As the centuries passed and power passed from Lithuanian to Polish hands, Orthodoxy firmly remained the religion of the peasants of Belarus. In 1917 the religion was swept away in the reforms of the Russian revolution, but it has seen a strong revival in recent years.

The Eastern Orthodox Church affirms seven mysteries or sacraments: baptism, anointing with holy oil, communion, holy orders, penance, anointing the sick, and marriage. Unlike the Catholic Church, where children are baptized but not confirmed in the faith until about age 7, the Eastern faith baptizes and confirms each child at the same time so that infants can take part in communion.

The marriage ceremony symbolizes eternal union between husband and wife. Remarriage after divorce is possible in Eastern Orthodoxy, but only on the understanding that the original union was not entered into effectively and that the vows were not taken seriously.

Fasting is an important part of Eastern Orthodoxy, much more so than in the other branches of Christianity. Fasting takes place on several occasions: Lent, the Fast of the Apostles in June, the Assumption in August, and in the period before Christmas. Fasting rules include giving up meat and animal products as well as wine and oil.

Prayer is a public activity in the Orthodox Church. While private prayer is also part of the religion, the prayers are the same as those recited in church and in monasteries. It is this sense of a community of worshipers rather than individuals that distinguishes the beliefs of this Church from Catholicism.

The bishop is always unmarried or widowed but the priests and deacons are allowed to marry, unlike in the Catholic Church.

In modern Belarus many people are rediscovering Eastern Orthodoxy. There are about 800 Orthodox congregations and Belarus has been designated an exarchate of the Russian Orthodox Church, meaning that it is a new branch of the church with its own bishop. In 1990, 60% of the population considered themselves to be Orthodox Christians. There is now a seminary for trainee priests, three convents, and a monastery in Belarus.

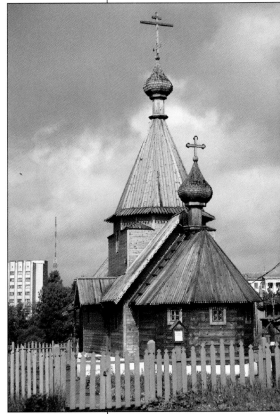

Above and opposite: **Two Orthodox churches: a traditional one in Vitebsk made mostly of wood and the striking onion domes of a church in Brest.**

A congregation arriving at a Catholic church in Grodno.

ROMAN CATHOLICISM

Roman Catholicism became a significant religion in Belarus during the time when Belarus was part of Greater Lithuania. Greater Lithuania formed a union in the 14th century with Poland, a firmly Roman Catholic country. As a result of the union, a strong Roman Catholic influence appeared in Belarus, largely through the Polish-speaking people in the west of the country. Many of the aristocrats were Roman Catholics, while the peasants were mostly Eastern Orthodox.

The Roman Catholic Church accepts the Pope as its head. All priests take a vow of celibacy and women are not allowed into the priesthood. Divorce, contraception, and abortion are all forbidden by the Church. Prayer is mostly a private communication between the individual and God.

About 20% of the population of Belarus is Roman Catholic: three quarters of this group are ethnic Poles, and a quarter are Belarusian. There is some conflict in Belarus between the Polish Catholic Church and the Belarusian Catholic Church over the language of the service. Most Catholic services are conducted in Polish, although Pope John Paul II has conducted services in Belarusian. There are more than

80 Catholic priests in Belarus, all of them Polish in origin. In 1989 the first Belarusian Bishop was consecrated, Tadeusz Kondrusiewicz, a Belarus-born Pole.

THE UNIATE CHURCH

The presence of both Eastern Orthodoxy and Roman Catholicism has resulted in severe conflict between the two churches. In 1595 an attempt was made to solve the problems by creating the Uniate Church. It used Belarusian as the language of services, adopted Orthodox doctrine, but acknowledged the Roman Catholic Pope as the head of the Church. It had little success with the mass of the population and became the tool of various political groups until it was banned altogether in 1839. Since 1990 attempts have been made to re-establish the church, which has many branches outside Belarus.

A branch of the Uniate Church exists in Toronto, Canada. In 1992 the leader of the Toronto Uniate Church, Mikalaj, came to visit the Uniate Church community in Minsk.

PROBLEMS BETWEEN THE RELIGIONS

In a country where choosing which language to speak is a major topic, the newly flowering churches have also become embroiled in political issues. The Roman Catholic Church is considered to be essentially Polish, but at least a quarter of Catholics are Belarusian. Most Catholic services are conducted in Polish, and Polish flags fly in many Catholic churches. Many Belarusians live in Bielastok inside Poland and are Orthodox Christians. Some claim that they are discriminated against in a region that Belarusian politicians have suggested is more Belarusian in character than Polish.

Meanwhile, in Orthodox churches, services are conducted in Russian and the head of the new regional head for Belarus is a Russian, Metropolitan Filaret. For many Belarusians with strong nationalist feelings this situation is unsatisfactory. To remedy the situation Metropolitan Filaret has commissioned a translation of the Bible into modern Belarusian and has included Belarusian festivals on the religious calendar.

This statue of Frances Skaryna, a famous 16th century humanist, stands in his birthplace, Polotsk.

IMPORTANT CHURCH FIGURES

FRANCES SKARYNA   Born in 1492 in Polotsk, Frances Skaryna translated and published the first Bible written in the Belarusian language. He was a humanist rather than a religious leader, but it was his translation of the Bible that made its words available to the peasants of Belarus for the first time. He was an important figure in the Renaissance with wide interests including theology, botany, poetry, law, art, and medicine. In 1530, after a fire that destroyed his printing presses, he went to Prussia and served as the doctor for the Duke of Prussia for a while. In his later years he became a gardener to the King of Bohemia.

SAINT EFRASINNIA OF POLOTSK   Born in 1110, Saint Efrasinnia was the granddaughter of Prince Useslau, the Magician of Polotsk. She felt she had a vocation from an early age and, refusing all offers of marriage, ran off to her aunt's convent. She later founded her own convent and was joined by other female members of her family. She further founded a monastery for monks and was abbess of both institutions. One of her occupations was to make copies of religious works that she then sold to give alms to the poor. She died in 1167 during a pilgrimage to the Holy Land in Jerusalem and her remains were carried back to Kiev, Ukraine, where they were buried in the Monastery of the Caves. They were finally returned to Polotsk in 1910. The Church of the Holy Savior, which she had built, still stands in Polotsk. She is an important figure today in the Eastern Orthodox Church.

OTHER RELIGIONS IN BELARUS

JUDAISM Jewish communities have existed in Belarus since the 14th century. By 1914 Jews made up about 14% of the population, living largely in the cities. In some places they formed 50% of the population. As a result of the genocide of World War II and consequent emigration, Jews are now only around 1% of the population.

The rabbi is the spiritual leader of the Jewish people. Worship in the home is just as important as worship in the synagogue and the religion lays down strict rules about worship. The Jewish Sabbath is from Friday evening to Saturday evening.

One branch of Judaism, about 250,000 strong, was founded in Belarus by Rabbi Schneur Zalmon in 1798. It runs 1,300 Hebrew schools and other institutions around the world.

Since independence there has been a flowering of Judaism in Belarus. Although many people are emigrating to Israel, others are rediscovering their roots and the customs of their religion. There is a yeshiva or Jewish seminary in Belarus, and many Jewish Sunday schools are being opened to teach Hebrew and the Talmud. About 70 Jewish organizations are active in Belarus. Despite all this, surveys show that a large proportion of the 10,000 Jews in Belarus have little or no connection with their cultural or religious roots. Some estimates suggest that if the current rate of emigration continues there will be no Jewish community in Belarus within 20 years.

ISLAM There is a small number of Muslims living in Belarus, mostly Tatars who settled in Belarus around the 11th century. Some of the first Belarusian texts were actually written phonetically in Arabic by Muslim priests.

Like other religions in Belarus, Islam also suffered suppression during the Soviet years. However, in 1939, the highest religious authority, the supreme Muslim council, was re-established.

Along with Orthodoxy and Catholicism, small groups of Protestants practice their religion in Belarus. There are about 200 Baptist churches and 350 Protestant congregations in total.

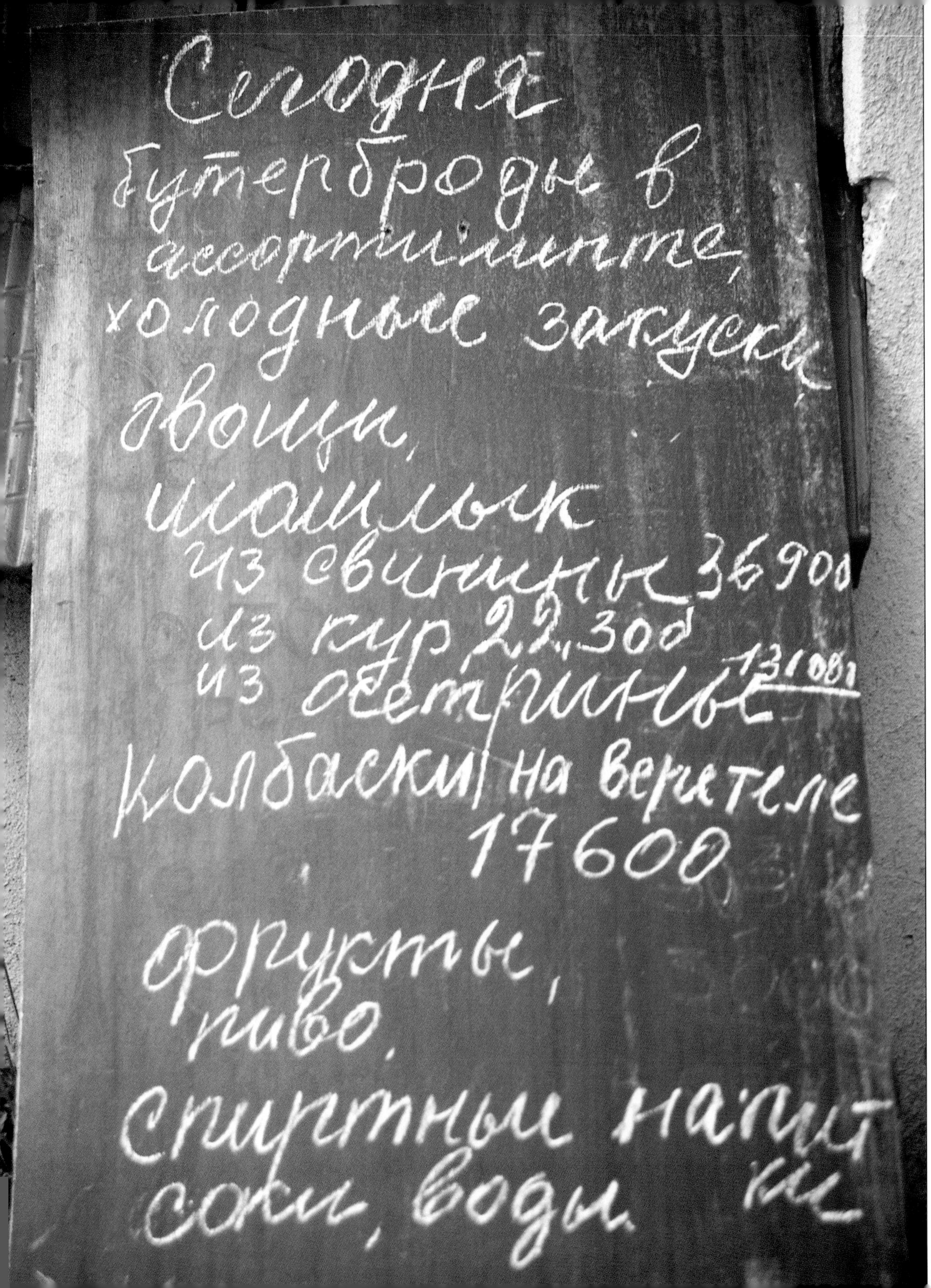

Сегодня

бутерброды в ассортименте,
холодные закуски,
овощи,
шашлык
из свинины 36900
из кур 22300б
из осетрины 131000
колбаски на вертеле
17600

фрукты,
пиво,
спиртные напитки
соки, воды.

LANGUAGE

WHEN THE NEWSPAPER *Zviadia* greeted its readers on New Year's Day 1992, its message was printed in five languages—Belarusian, Russian, Polish, Yiddish, and Ukrainian. Except for the last, all these languages were in official use in the liberal early years of the Soviet Union.

In modern times, the Russian language is dominant. While Belarus was part of the Russian empire, as well as when it was part of the USSR, the Belarusian language was discouraged and finally banned outright. The language has suffered greatly as a result. It is still in use, but it is an endangered language and only 11% of the population, mostly those in rural areas, speak it fluently.

Above: **These posters are in Russian.**

Opposite: **A menu for a restaurant. Russian and Belarusian are both written in the Cyrillic script.**

The first signs of perestroika or reform in Belarus came in 1986 when a group of intellectuals wrote to Mikhail Gorbachev, the leader of the USSR, asking for the country's language to be recognized. Shortly before independence, in 1990, Belarusian was declared the national language and a period of 10 years was decided on until it became the main language to be used in public life. Street signs were changed to Belarusian, Both languages are now used in schools.

Yiddish, spoken by the Jewish community, has become a minority language since World War II and the Stalinist era. Only a few still speak it at home. Polish is also a minority language and is spoken primarily in Catholic church services. The language of the Tatars is a Turkic one and although the number of Tatar people in Belarus is low, the language is still spoken. During Stalin's era their language was forbidden throughout the USSR. Since the break-up of the Soviet central government many Tatar people throughout the former USSR have taken the opportunity to return to the Crimea, their former home.

EARLY ROOTS OF LANGUAGE

The University of Polotsk. It was closed down temporarily in the late 1800s when the Russian empire banned the Belarusian language.

By the 13th century, the language used in the Grand Duchy of Lithuania was the Belarusian language. It was used in all official matters and was spoken by most of the population. In 1569 the Treaty of Lublin merged Lithuania with Poland and a gradual process of "Polonization" began. Polish became the language of the court and the Catholic Church, while the peasantry spoke Belarusian. Between the 14th and 16th centuries the written form of Belarusian developed, using the Cyrillic alphabet. Frances Skaryna published works in Belarusian followed by Symon Budny, Simeon Polotsky, and many others. Belarusian became the dynamic force in printing and its translations from Latin were used to produce Russian and Polish texts.

In the 18th century, the region of Belarus was incorporated into the Russian empire and the process of Russification began. The Belarusian language was suppressed and Russian became the language of the courts, administration, and church. In 1864 all Belarusian publications were banned, schools were closed, and the University of Polotsk was shut down. Belarusian became the language of the illiterate peasants, while education and a career required Russian.

The fortunes of the Belarusian language improved after the Belorussian Soviet Socialist Republic was declared under Soviet rule in 1919. Dissidents returned from Europe and began writing in their native language, schools and universities were reopened, and teaching and publishing took place in Belarusian.

But by the late 1920s, the period of tolerance was over and the process of Russification began again. Teacher training was in Russian, so new teachers taught only in that language. As elderly Belarusian teachers retired, the language disappeared with them. By the late 1980s, there was not a single school in the capital, Minsk, using any Belarusian. Russian became the language of commerce, education, government, even conversation in factories. While illiteracy was virtually eradicated and educational standards grew as quickly as economic security, it was at the cost of the Belarusian language.

Then, in 1990, just before independence, Belarusian was declared the national language. Street signs were changed back to Belarusian and the language was reintroduced into classrooms. But for many people this was going too far too fast. Russian was the most commonly spoken language. Many parents were reluctant to see their children educated in a minority language that no one outside Belarus could use. In 1995 a referendum made both Russian and Belarusian national languages.

Both Russian and Belarusian are now taught in schools, a change from the days under the USSR when only Russian was used.

The first written use of the Belarusian language was in early Tatar religious texts, using Arabic letters but Belarusian words.

THE POLITICS OF LANGUAGE

Belarus and Russia are currently negotiating a political union of the two countries. Many people in both countries oppose this. President Lukashenko's politics are very right-wing and he has praised both Stalin and Hitler. Not many Russian people would want a return to that kind of state.

Language has become a part of more complex issues such as choosing between independence and union or between free markets and communism. Many intellectuals believe that the Belarusian culture is enshrined in the language and that if the language dies, there will no longer be a Belarus and the place will simply be a region of Russia.

For other people the issue is simpler. They have learned Russian all their lives and see it as a means of advancement. They remember the good times of the Soviet Union when there were benefits such as full employment. Many want these benefits back. They feel that there is little point in trying to use a language that no one really speaks fluently, especially when they already have another language (that is, Russian) that works perfectly well.

BELARUSIAN

Belarusian is an east Slavic language, closely related to both Russian and Ukrainian. The Slavs who first moved into the area spread around the eastern Europe region carrying their language with them. As they settled, their language merged with the indigenous languages. There are now around 11 Slavic languages divided into three groups. Russian, Belarusian, and Ukrainian are all in the same group and have many common words.

Belarusian, like Russian, is written in the Cyrillic alphabet. This alphabet originated in the 9th century when a Greek missionary, Cyril, adapted the Greek alphabet to produce the scriptures in Slavic languages. Originally the alphabet had 43 characters, but the many languages that make use of the alphabet have adapted it to their own needs. Belarusian can also be written in a Roman form, but this is rarely used.

Many Belarusian words are Russian words with slightly different spellings and pronunciations. Belarusian has also borrowed from Polish, a quite unrelated Slavic language. In other ways, Belarusian is closer to Ukrainian. Both languages have a vowel pronounced "ee" where there is no such sound in Russian. Belarusian also has a unique letter pronounced like the English *w* as in "wait."

Of several regional dialects of Belarusian, the most significantly different is the one spoken in Pinsk. People from Pinsk call themselves *Pinchuki* ("pin-CHOOK-ee") after the area where they live and speak a dialect that has many words and expressions not found in standard Belarusian. They consider theirs to be a different language from Belarusian, and many believe the Pinsk language and culture to have different origins from the rest of Belarus.

Often encyclopedias and other books have different spellings for the same name or place in Belarus. Many of these variations are a result of one book using a Russian form of the word while another uses the Belarusian form. For example, the town sometimes spelled as Grodno is often spelled as Hrodno. Similarly, Gomel may be spelled Homel. This is because in Russian the Cyrillic character is pronounced as a hard *g* while the same character in Belarusian is pronounced as *h*. President Lukashenko's name is spelled as Lukashenka when transliterated using the Belarusian pronunciation. Even "Belarus" can be spelled in many different ways!

In the cities most people speak Russian and not Belarusian. A 1992 survey revealed that the majority believed bilingualism to be the way forward, and only 17% wanted Belarusian to be the only state language.

CYRILLIC	TRANSLIT-ERATION	PRONUNCIATION	CYRILLIC	TRANSLIT-ERATION	PRONUNCIATION
А	a	Father	Р	r	ravioli (rolled r)
Б	b	bit	С	s	Soviet
В	v	vote	Т	t	ten
Г	g	goat	У	u	pool
Д	d	dog	Ф	f	fit
Е	ye	yes	Х	kh	Bach
Ё	yo	yoke	Ц	ts	cats
Ж	zh	azure	Ч	ch	cheer
З	z	zero	Ш	sh	shop
И	i	feet	Щ	shch	fresh sheets
Й	y	boy	Ъ		hardens following vowel
К	k	kit	Ы	y	shrill
Л	l	let	Ь		softens preceding consonant
М	m	map	Э	e	bed
Н	n	not	Ю	yu	cute
О	o	owe	Я	ya	yacht
П	p	pat			

RUSSIAN

Russian is the most widely spoken language in Belarus. Like Belarusian, it uses the Cyrillic alphabet, although some of its characters are different. It has 33 characters and several of its sounds are completely unfamiliar to English speakers.

In many cases several English characters have to be used to represent one single Russian sound. For example, the Russian word for cabbage stew has two letters—щи—but must be represented in English by six letters—*shchee*.

A result of years of Russification in Belarus is the development of a new pidgin language that is a mixture of Belarusian and Russian grammar and vocabulary. This language is called *trasnyanka* ("traz-YAN-kah") and is spoken by at least half the population to varying degrees. It functions as a "bazaar Russian" spoken by people who have adopted Russian without officially learning the rules of the language.

WHAT'S IN A NAME?

If you have read other books or perhaps encyclopedias about Belarus you will have noticed that there are many spellings of the country's name. Bielorussia, Byelorussia, White Russia, Belorussia, and Belarus are a few of the ways to write it in English. In the past it was part of Lithuania (now a completely different country), while under Russian imperial rule it was part of western Russia and the name Belarus was banned altogether.

The literal translation is "White Russia" after the ancient term *Belaya Rus.* Many suggestions have been made for the origin of the word Belaya or "white." It might refer to the beauty of the countryside or the vast quantities of snow in the area. One suggestion is that the word white means "free" and was used for the part of Belarus that was not invaded by the Tatars. The word Rus comes from the area of land formed by a triangle of three cities—Kiev, Chernigov, and Pereyaslaval (all in modern Ukraine). It is probably the same root word as in "Russia," and was used to refer to all Orthodox Christians. As the Tatars (who were Muslims) took over the Ukraine, the center of Christian Orthodoxy became Moscow and so the name, Rus, moved with the religion.

People attending a book fair in Belarus.

While Belarus was part of the USSR, the official spelling in English was Byelorussia. After independence it was called, in Belarusian, *Respublika Bielarus,* which was turned into *Belarus* by the Western media. Nationalists prefer the spelling Belarus since it distances the country from Russia; those in favor of union with Russia prefer the older spelling.

ARTS

OVER THE CENTURIES Belarusian culture and arts have flourished and declined in turn. The Renaissance saw a flourishing of architecture and literature, while the 19th century and early 20th century were also good times for Belarusian culture. Belarusian emigres have also contributed to the arts in their new homes.

During the Soviet era the Socialist Realism school of art and architecture was popular. Crafts, folk songs, folk dances, and music of all kinds survived the various changes and misfortunes that have occurred throughout Belarus's history, and poetry and theater have remained an important part of life for everyone. Yiddish literature also prospered in Belarus and many famous Jewish figures in the United States media and arts had their beginnings in this little-known backwater of the Russian empire. Marc Chagall, a particularly well-known artist who was originally from Belarus, used his home town as a theme in many of his paintings.

Left: **Students at a secondary school of art in Bobruisk.**

Opposite: **Pottery figures of birds, animals, and people are popular folk art. They are brightly glazed and used as ornaments in the home or as toys for children.**

A group of musicians in traditional clothes and felt hats.

MUSIC

Belarus has a long tradition of folk music, which was encouraged during the Soviet era. The Christian Orthodox Church also has a long tradition of music performed by choirs. Folk music includes special songs for weddings, comic songs, dance tunes, and ballads about past heroes. Several choirs perform internationally and there is an orchestra dedicated to folk music. Typical instruments of Belarusian folk music are cymbals, pipes, accordions, lyres, and balalaikas, which are triangle-shaped string instruments, a little like guitars.

Opera and ballet are very popular in Belarus and state opera and ballet companies perform regularly. Belarusian composers such as Yuri Semenyako, Yevgeny Glebov, and Heinrich Wagner have produced operas in musical versions of the Socialist Realist style.

Pop music also flourishes in Belarus with Belarusian versions of the bands that are popular in St. Petersburg, Russia. They are not known outside of Belarus, but thrive in the music scene in the cities.

ARCHITECTURE

Ancient buildings are the oldest examples of art in many countries and even in war-torn Belarus a few ancient buildings have survived. The earliest surviving style of architecture is very simple and can be seen in the 12th century church of Saints Boris and Gleb in Grodno, with its curved, stone apse. A church from the 11th century also survives, the Cathedral of St. Sophia in Polotsk. It was damaged by fire in the 15th century, however, and in the 18th century was remodeled in the Baroque style. This highly elaborate Baroque style was brought to Belarus under Polish domination in the 17th and 18th centuries.

In the 18th century a Classical style of architecture with simple lines and minimal decoration was preferred. There was a brief cultural revival in the early 20th century when architects sought to use the traditional folk styles of simple peasant houses, but this quickly gave way to the grand buildings of Stalin's era and a rejection of the various cultures of the Soviet Union. The school of Soviet Classicism was a grandiose style with tiers of stonework and ornate columns all designed to create a sense of power and greatness. The style took earlier ideas and exaggerated them in size and design.

In the late 20th century, house architecture has been simple in design. After World War II, thousands of people needed to be rehoused quickly and large satellite towns were built with high-rise apartment buildings made from prefabricated materials. To soften the starkness of these buildings the surroundings were turned into parkland.

The elaborate spire of an Orthodox cathedral in Grodno.

89

The screen in front of the altar is called an iconostasis and is covered with elaborately painted icons, or miniature portraits. This iconostasis is from an Orthodox church in Minsk.

RELIGIOUS ICONS

One of the most ancient forms of art in Belarus is religious icons. These are miniature paintings of religious figures such as the Virgin Mary, other figures from the Bible, or various saints. The Eastern Orthodox Church does not allow three-dimensional figures such as statues so icons are the main way of decorating churches. Icon painting spread from Byzantium (modern-day Turkey) to eastern Europe and Russia in the 14th century and was used in Belarus both in churches and the home. Simple portraits of religious figures are used as the centerpiece of an altar in the home, while in the churches more elaborate, gilded portraits are used. In the Middle Ages most peasants were illiterate so icons also served as religious storybooks.

In Belarus, icon painting changed over the centuries to include elements from Belarusian folk art and mythology. Often the saints are depicted wearing Belarusian national costume. Common domestic icon illustrations are St. George and the dragon and St. Nicholas.

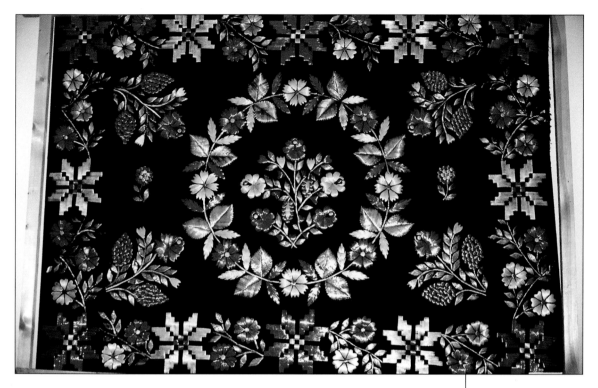

CRAFTS, WOODCARVING, AND CERAMICS

Outside the religious context, art remained primarily a folk tradition until the late 19th century. Woodcarving was a particularly impressive Belarusian skill. In the 15th century the Russian tsar, Ivan the Terrible, employed Belarusian carpenters and woodcarvers in the construction of his palaces and churches. Another folk art tradition was ceramic and carved wooden toys. The wooden figures were highly elaborate with jointed limbs and delicate, painted faces.

Working in straw is also a very old tradition. Boxes and figures are made out of intricately inlaid or woven straw. The most distinctive form of craftwork in Belarus is embroidery on items such as towels, blouses, pinafores, and skirts in the traditional styles. The cloths and towels are used for decoration in the home. They are collected by young girls about to marry and carefully stored, to be aired on special occasions such as weddings and family parties. Amber is crafted into jewelry and is worn with traditional clothing.

Embroidered articles have many uses in Belarusian culture. They may be used in weddings or as decoration in the home.

MARC CHAGALL

Vitebsk's most famous citizen must be Marc Chagall. He was born in 1887 when Vitebsk was part of the Russian empire. He came from a modest Jewish family of eight children and went to a Jewish primary school and a Russian language secondary school. He studied art under a local Realist artist, Yehuda Pen, and then went to St. Petersburg to study more formally.

Chagall's painted his early works before the period of the Surrealist school of art but they are very much in a surreal style. He abandoned Realist rules about logic in pictures, painting instead a reality more psychological than real. He spent some years in Europe studying with other bohemian artists and poets and under their encouraging influence developed his whimsical style. Many of his paintings were images from his home life in Vitebsk. He returned to Vitebsk in 1914 and married a local Jewish girl named Bella Rosenfeld. He started painting in more of a Realist style again, and his wife appears in many of his paintings.

Chagall enthusiastically joined in the October Revolution in 1917 and became the commissar for art at the local academy and museum. But gradually he became disillusioned with the revolution and left first for Moscow and then left Russia and Belarus forever. In Europe and the United States he became a very popular artist, producing huge canvasses of dreamlike subject matter in rich colors. He finally settled in Paris and the themes of his Vitebsk life gradually faded out of his work. He died in 1985.

SOCIALIST REALISM

Marc Chagall abandoned his native land at the same time that Socialist Realism became the official Soviet art style. In the West, avant-garde art was the dominant art form, with painters expressing emotion rather than making photographic reproductions of what they saw. But in the USSR, Soviet authorities saw art as a form of propaganda, that is, a way of teaching the population about socialism. In 1934 Socialist Realism was declared the official style for communist art. The subject matter was to be about the creation of the socialist state.

Initially the art was optimistic in tone, showing handsome, finely muscled heroes of the revolution building new factories and working on the land, but toward the 1960s it developed a bleaker, less realistic style, taking ideas from the avant-garde and showing personal images as well as public scenes. Belarus's public places filled with such paintings as well as great statues and monuments aimed at showing the grandeur of socialism. As the Soviet Union began to disintegrate, these statues were the first to disappear all over the USSR and eastern Europe. Later the paintings were taken down and replaced with reproductions of impressionists or even Chagall's work.

Many Belarusian artists contributed to the years of Socialist Realism. One, Mikhail Savitsky, is well known for his painting *Partisan Madonna* and received the silver medal of the Union of Soviet Artists. Another famous painter is Mark Danzig who painted *My Town* and *Belarus—The Partisan's Mother*. Other painters of renown are Zair Azgur, Leonid Shemelev, and Andrei Bembel.

Paintings in the Socialist Realist style were common throughout the Soviet Union for many years. They were forms of propaganda and usually depicted the ideally strong, productive, and dauntless worker or farmer.

Yakub Kolas is a poet and novelist, and one of the founders of modern Belarusian literature.

LITERATURE

Printing and writing was highly developed in Belarus long before the rest of the Slavic world. Frances Skaryna was publishing in the Belarusian language in the early 16th century and was followed 50 years later by Symon Budny, Vasil Cyapinski, and others. In the 17th century, Simeon Polotsky wrote the first poetry in Belarusian. The 19th century saw a cultural renaissance in Belarusian literature. The popular anonymous poem *Taras on Parnassus* is about a peasant who accidentally finds himself in the home of the gods who are living just like peasants. The poem stands out as a landmark in Belarusian literature as it pointedly suggested that the real heart of poetry lay in the folk culture, not the Russian intellectual elite that dominated Belarusian life at the time.

Under the Russian empire however, all use of the Belarusian language was banned and publishing was prohibited. Writing continued but was published abroad and under pseudonyms. In 1905 life became a little more liberated under the Russians, and writers again were able to publish in their own language. Two of Belarus's greatest novelists, Yanka Kupala and Yakub Kolas, wrote during this period.

In modern times literature continues to flourish in Belarus. A union of Belarusian writers was formed in 1932 to support writers although only politically acceptable works were allowed. Vasil Bykov is now a leading political figure but is best known as a writer. Other renowned modern writers are Vladimir Karatkevich, Anatol Sys, and Ales Razanov.

TWO BELARUSIAN WRITERS

YANKA KUPALA was born in 1882 under the name Ivan Lucevic, in a small village in central Belarus, to peasant farmers. He spent his early years traveling with his family in search of work. Early tragedies in his life made him the head of the family at a young age. He had little education and most of his knowledge came from books in the private library of a friend.

Lucevic's first efforts at writing were poetry in Polish, but in 1905 he published a series of poems about the lives of peasants. He adopted the pseudonym Yanka Kupala and became a leading member of the group of writers for the magazine *Nasa Niva*. His body of work includes nature and love poetry, works on social and national themes, four plays, and dramatic and narrative poetry. His work declined in the years of Stalin but his peak work is considered the greatest in Belarus. He died in 1942.

YAKUB KOLAS Considered the cofounder of modern Belarusian literature, Kanstancin Mickievic was born into a peasant family in 1882 in a small village near Minsk. Growing up in the countryside had a profound effect on his work. The family was literate and Mickievic was educated by his uncle. At first he read in Russian, but later he discovered Belarusian poetry. He attended teacher-training college and his first efforts at poetry were in Russian. His first prose work, using the name Yakub Kolas, was in his local dialect and was about his home village.

As Yakub Kolas learned and read more, he became a revolutionary and was dismissed from college. He wrote a reader for children and went to Vilnius where the magazine *Nasa Niva* was published. His poetry was quite political and satirical at times but he also wrote poetry about nature and peasant life. He went on to write novels and allegorical short stories. He continued producing good work for many years, even in the repressive years of Stalin's rule.

Yanka Kupala's play, The Locals, *provides critical insights into Belarusian culture under the strain of war and revolution.*

LEISURE

LEISURE IN BELARUS is a mixture of traditional cultural entertainment in rural areas and more sophisticated modern attractions in the cities. Some traditional activities were encouraged during the Soviet era as were sports. In modern times all the attractions of the West are beamed in on satellite television. In its search for tourist dollars, Belarus is also encouraging activities such as trekking and wildlife watching. New and less restrictive rules about travel mean that now people can visit parts of the world they have never before seen.

The way people spend their free time in Belarus depends a great deal on their income and work commitment. For some people the new economic circumstances have brought unemployment and increased leisure time but no money to spend. For others, the challenge of a new free-market economy means there are fortunes to be made but little time or opportunity to enjoy their new wealth.

Left: **A horseman practices his skills at a water jump.**

Opposite: **Children at a playground on a collective farm.**

IN THE OUTDOORS

When new cities were planned in the 1950s and 1960s, the architects were well aware of the disadvantages of city life. Most suburban areas are therefore set in green belts with lots of open space and parks for children to play in. Outside the cities, buildings give way to the Belarusian countryside of fields, forests, lakes, and rivers. The countryside is quite beautiful and very distinctive with vast golden cornfields or huge fields of flax that are bright blue in the summer. With no seacoast, the lakes provide beaches for sunbathing, picnics, and swimming and more luxurious sports such as water-skiing and sailing. One very popular spot for residents of Minsk is the Minsk Sea, a dam and reservoir near the city. It is surrounded by woodland walks and picnic areas and is very popular on weekends. Fishing is a popular activity too.

Both lakes and rivers in Belarus are full of edible fish. These people are trying their luck in the Pripet River.

COUNTRY HOUSES

In the old days of the Russian empire, the upper classes had a special home in the country called a *dacha* ("DAH-chah") where they would go when the summer in Moscow got too hot or they felt like a rest. Even under the Soviet Union, the *dachas* remained special places for the elite who were the communist party officials. Because of its vast forests and good hunting, Belarus has many such *dachas* located in the countryside. High-ranking Soviet officials would often spend time at them. Several major political treaties of the 1960s and 1970s were in fact signed in Belarusian country houses. Other *dachas* have over time been turned into sanatoria or vacation resorts.

People enjoy camping in forest reserves. Hunting is a sport that also provides a major source of the meat eaten in Belarus. The forests are so full of wildlife that unlike other countries that have to protect their forest animals, Belarus can organize hunting tourism. Another favorite activity is picking fruit in the forest. Most people recognize edible mushrooms and berries and a whole family might spend the day picking the ingredients for next month's jams, jellies, and mushroom stews.

Friends may set up a game of chess in one of the parks if the weather is pleasant.

Drum majorettes at a music festival. Such festivals are held in many of the cities and are a popular form of entertainment.

STORYTELLING AND THEATER

Leisure pursuits are different for people who live in the country rather than in the cities. What city folk might see as a hobby, country people usually view as work. In the historical period they had little time for leisure. The evening would be spent in weaving or preparing preserves or sewing. While involved in these activities the family and their guests would chat, share the news, and tell stories.

Storytelling was an important part of Belarusian life before television and is still part of Belarusian culture. Belarusians know many *kaski* ("KAH-ski"), satirical moral stories that illustrate some aspect of life. There is a story for every occasion. Children have always been taught their lessons about life in this indirect way. The nature of these stories tells us a lot about the Belarusian character and outlook on life.

There was also a long tradition of traveling theaters in the Belarusian countryside. Ukrainian theater groups were already traveling around in Belarus with comic stories long before the establishment of The Belarusian Traveling Theater in the 1920s. The most popular entertainment was comic shows or melodramas. Audience participation was a lively part of the show, with the audience shouting "look out, he's behind you" in true vaudeville fashion as the villain crept up on the hero. One person who attended a show tells how a character in the play searched in his pockets for a cigarette and a member of the audience actually jumped up and gave him one!

TWO BELARUSIAN STORIES

Belarusians love to tell stories about the supernatural. In many peasant communities people believe in elves and spirits, and Slav tales about vampires have their place in Belarusian mythology. Here are two tales:

THE WOMAN AND HER CHILD   There was once a woman who had grown very tired of constantly carrying her children in her arms. She went to the Great Magician and complained that children cannot walk until they are more than a year old, while lambs, calves, and foals can all walk right after they are born. The Great Magician said that he would help her. He first took a foal and threw it over the hedge. The foal jumped to its feet and ran away. Then he took a lamb and threw it over the hedge. The same thing happened—the lamb got up and gamboled away. Next it was the calf's turn.

Then the magician turned to the woman. "Hand over your child," he ordered. The woman was outraged. "How dare you suggest I throw my child over the fence," she shouted and stormed off in a huff. The magician shrugged and went on his way.

HOW A VAMPIRE CARRIED A GIRL OFF TO THE GRAVE   A young girl and boy very much in love made vows to remain faithful to one another. "If I marry another, let the devil take me," announced the girl.

A year later, another young man came by her house and started to pay her compliments. He was richer and handsomer than her lover, and the girl broke her engagement and promised to marry her new lover. On the evening before the wedding a vampire turned up disguised in the shape of her former suitor. "Come outside with me, I want to tell you something," he said to the girl. She followed him out and saw a saddled horse. He pulled her up on to the horse and rode away. "There are vampires out tonight. Are you afraid?" he asked. She laughed. "Of course not," she said. A little later he asked again and she denied being afraid again. Then he told her who he was. They came to some graves and one of them was standing open. The vampire said, "Do you remember your promise? Well, you have broken it and now I have come for you as you vowed." He unscrewed her head and threw it down into the grave, then he followed it down into the earth.

This story has a moral warning not to break promises. The vampire does not suck the girl's blood but takes away the offending part of her.

Belarusian stories often include vampires. Their vampires, unlike those in Western horror movies, take on different shapes and have pacts with the devil. They may not suck blood, but they do live in graves and may commit various horrifying deeds such as cutting off a person's head!

ENTERTAINMENT IN THE CITIES

There are many things to do in the cities in one's free time. Transportation into the cities is relatively cheap and in town there are movies and theaters, puppet shows, museums, and cafés that sell alcohol as well as food and are open until late at night. In Minsk alone the Yanka Kupala Theater, the Russian Drama Theater, the Minsk Puppet Theater, and the State Theater of Musical Comedy are all very popular. Most restaurants have bands or even small orchestras, and a night out with dinner and dancing is a popular evening activity.

For young people there are discos and music clubs, and pizza joints selling foreign beer. Most pop music in Belarus is in Russian, but there are local bands such as Mroja, Ulis, and Bonda which are also popular in Belarus. The organization called Next Stop-New Life arranges youth festivals, cultural exchanges, and summer camps for young people. There are also many sports stadiums where people can take part in sports or watch games.

SPORTS

Sports are taken very seriously in Belarus. In addition to many opportunities for watching sports, there are 478 sports schools; 120 are dedicated to the Olympic sports. There are also eight colleges dedicated to sports. Cross-country skiing is a very popular weekend activity in a country where there is snow cover for over six months of the year. There are several successful basketball players in Belarus, four of whom are currently studying on scholarships in the United States. Alexander Koul, in particular, may well be drafted into the National Basketball Association (NBA). In tennis, Vladimir Voltchkov won the 1996 Junior Wimbledon. Two women tennis players also stand out—Olga Barabanschikova and Natasha Zvereva. The latter has won several titles playing in doubles with Gigi Fernandez.

Young boys playing football in Minsk. Belarus's most successful football team is Dinamo Minsk. It has a large modern stadium and often hosts international matches.

Belarusians have excelled in the Olympic sports. Olga Korbut and Nelli Kim, both world renowned names in gymnastics, are from Belarus while the two strongest men in the world, Alexander Kurlovich and Leonid Taranenko, are also Belarusian. In the Barcelona Olympics, in 1992, Belarusian athletes claimed 17 gold, 4 silver, and 6 bronze medals.

In the Atlanta Olympics in 1996, Belarus competed for the second time as a country and did very well. Many of the athletes competed wearing the red and white colors of the newly independent state, while others wore the colors of the old Soviet flag. The great athlete Vitaly Scherbo, winner of six Olympic gold medals and a total of 14 world gold medals, won four bronze medals for gymnastics, the horizontal bar, the parallel bars, and the vault. Other Belarusian athletes also won medals.

THE MEDIA

In Belarus, 93% of the population owns a television set and some may own two or three. Only 15% of the population has access to satellite or cable television and about 10% own a VCR.

Belarusian people watch their own national TV channel, which is state owned, as well as Russian TV channels. Of these one is an independent channel. The Russian independent channel received in Belarus, NTV, includes in its programs investigative news shows as well as political debates but for the most part news is presented by state television. Belarusian television broadcasts in a mixture of Belarusian and Russian. In the southern and western parts of the country viewers can pick up Polish and Ukrainian stations. A few people have access to satellite television or cable but most of these programs are in foreign languages. The chief barrier to ownership of a satellite is the high cost of the equipment rather than lack of interest in the service.

Watching television has become a major daily activity just as it has in the West. Several Western soap operas and situation comedies have found

FILMS BY YURI KHASHCHEVATSKY

These days, under President Lukashenko, the government has begun banning the work of many poets, journalists, and filmmakers whose work criticizes the government and its policies. One of the leading filmmakers in Belarus is Yuri Khashchevatsky. He studied at the film academy in St. Petersburg, Russia. His most recent film, *An Ordinary President*, is a non-flattering documentary about President Lukashenko and has been banned in Belarus. It is immensely popular though and has been circulating underground in the country.

The movie poster in Minsk advertising the screening of *Werewolf* is dramatic enough to draw anyone in to see the film.

their way onto Belarusian TV screens. Satellite television is uncensored, unlike state channels. Programs tend to include lots of variety and cultural shows, movies, some foreign TV series, and news broadcasts. Russian and Belarusian soaps deal with similar themes to Western ones—love triangles, family relationships, and sometimes more challenging moral issues. Old Western movies are dubbed or subtitled and many young Belarusians are as interested in the lives of movie stars such as Stallone or Schwarzenegger as their counterparts in the United States. There are also two national radio stations, and of course many foreign radio stations can be received.

Around 460 newspapers and magazines are published in Belarus, of which about 150 are in Belarusian and a similar number in Russian. The rest are published in a mixture of the two languages or in the minority languages—Polish, Ukrainian, or English. State subsidies are given to magazines or newspapers published in Belarusian, or those involved in the arts or that publish for children. The most popular daily newspapers are *Sovetskaya Belorossiya*, *Dobry Vechar*, and *Narodnaya Hazeta*, published in Russian and Belarusian; while *Belorusskaya Niva* is published in Russian.

FESTIVALS

FOR THE 70 OR SO YEARS that Belarus was a part of the USSR, most of its traditional festivals were very quietly observed, if at all. In the early years of the Russian revolution, priests were tried and imprisoned, and Christian and other festivals publicly mocked. People attended the Soviet parades and other celebrations for the October Revolution. But the religions were never completely outlawed and the few churches and synagogues throughout the Soviet Union continued to observe the major festivals. Christian churches would ring church bells and many people would stand nearby to listen to them.

In modern Belarus, many people of all religions are rediscovering their roots and traditional festivals are reappearing once again. Pagan festivals that predate Christianity are still very popular today. They celebrate the seasons, for example, by welcoming spring or the summer solstice. Modern festivals in Belarus include music and arts festivals.

Left: **A group of women performing a traditional dance in a park.**

Opposite: **This mask of a sheep's head is worn during the traditional winter festival of Kaliady.**

TRADITIONAL FESTIVALS

Many festivals that date back to pre-Christian times are still celebrated in Belarus. The winter and summer solstice are very important.

People join hands and dance in a large circle around the bonfire during the Kupalle festival.

KUPALLE The festival of Kupalle ("koo-PAH-leh") is held around the summer solstice in June and sometimes in July and celebrates nature and summertime. It is thought to be named after a pagan goddess. People return to their home villages to celebrate out in the fields and forests, with picnics and bonfires. Traditional songs are sung and performed on ancient Belarusian instruments. People dance in *karagods* ("KAH-rah-gods"), circles around the bonfires. At this time, people also search for a particular fern that rarely flowers—if found, it is believed to bring good luck. There is a saying that if one falls in love during Kupalle, the marriage will be a very happy one.

KALIADY The winter solstice, Kaliady ("kal-ee-AD-ee"), is celebrated right before Christmas and is even more popular than Kupalle. Groups of young people dress up in traditional clothes and wear masks depicting animals, in particular, sheep. They carry a board with a sun on it, perhaps to remind everyone that the worst of the long, cold winter is over, and the sun will soon be strong again. The crowd of young people visit house to house, singing and dancing, and displaying the sheep's mask to the head of the household. Each house offers them food and drink in return.

HARVEST FESTIVAL Another ancient festival is the harvest festival, Dozinkyoi ("dozsh-INK-yah"), when people celebrate the successful completion of the harvest. People will travel home to their villages to join in the celebrations. A huge party is held where food from the hard summer's work on the farm is enjoyed, and the tables are decorated with buckets of flowers and herbs. Traditional songs are sung and people dance around bonfires.

TIDYING OF GRAVES Another ancient tradition in Belarus which pre-dates Christianity is the annual tidying of graves. It is celebrated at different times of the year by different groups. Catholics celebrate this on November 2, Remembrance Day, called Dzyady ("TSYAH-dee"). Orthodox Christians celebrate the festival at the Easter of the Dead, around April 23, called Radovniza ("RAH-doh-nit-sah"). At these times people travel to the graves of their parents and grandparents to tidy the graves, light candles, and to leave some food and drinks. Some families bring parts of their painted Easter eggs to the grave to show that the ancestor is still a part of the family. At the grandfather's grave some vodka is often left.

Yanka Kupala, a famous writer and poet in the 19th century, took his name from Kupalle since he was born at the time of the summer solstice.

A vigorous dance to celebrate Kaliady, the winter festival.

Christmas is calculated by a different calendar in the Orthodox Church, and is celebrated on January 7 instead of in December.

NATIONAL AND RELIGIOUS HOLIDAYS

January 1	New Year
January 7	Orthodox Christmas
March 8	Women's Day
March 15	Constitution Day
March/April	Catholic Easter
March/April	Orthodox Easter
April 23 (variable)	Easter of the Dead
May 1	Labor Day
May 9	Victory Day
June 21	Kupalle (solstice celebration)
July 27	Independence Day
November 2	Remembrance Day
November 7	October Revolution
December 21	Kaliady
December 25	Catholic Christmas

CHRISTIAN FESTIVALS

The Orthodox and Catholic Churches follow different calendars and so celebrate the religious holidays on different days. Easter is the most important religious occasion in the Orthodox Church. It is at least 13 days after the Catholic Easter. It must also always fall after the Jewish Passover festival. Easter is preceded by the long period of Lent which is a time of fasting in Eastern Orthodoxy.

The celebrations for Easter begin the week before Easter Sunday with a service of forgiveness. On Good Friday there is a procession of the

Epitahion ("ep-it-AH-hyon") or laying out of the body of Christ. The next service is the blessing of fire and a service of Vigil. But first a procession takes place that symbolizes the search for the body of Christ. The procession leaves the church in darkness but as it returns and the resurrection is announced, thousands of candles and lights are lit. The sacrament of communion is given early on Easter Sunday morning. Eastern Orthodox processions and services are highly ornate and elaborate events with the priests in elaborate costumes and icons and other holy paintings being carried.

Easter is a very important occasion for Catholics as well and is preceded by the long fast of Lent. On the day itself there are many colorful processions and people light candles to commemorate the resurrection.

The Catholic Christmas is celebrated in December, which is also the time for the traditional pre-Christian festival of Kaliady. Some of its customs have been absorbed into the Christmas celebration.

As in Orthodox Christianity, Catholic churches have tended to keep celebrations very low key and are still finding their own ways to begin celebrating again.

EASTER EGGS

While Easter is celebrated as a Christian festival, many ancient traditions are associated with it. Painted eggs are a very old Easter tradition, especially in eastern Europe, and go back to a time when the Easter festival celebrated the birth of a new season. Eggs symbolize new life. In the ancient religions this time of year would have been very important.

In Belarus, Easter is a time for the whole family to assemble at their parents' house for a big meal. A special round cake is baked and a single hen's egg is decorated in red. People take the egg and the cake to church to a special mass where they are blessed. Then, after the family meal, the egg and cake are cut up to give each member of the family an equal share to symbolize the unity of the family.

JEWISH FESTIVALS

The Jewish community today in Belarus is very small. During the Soviet era, many Jewish people played down their religion in order to avoid persecution. Today there is a revival of Judaism and many young people are seeking out the religious festivals of their culture. The feast of the Passover celebrates the ancient exodus of the Israelite tribe from Egypt. The festival lasts for eight days and begins with a family gathering for the Passover Seder. Prayers and songs are followed by a meal with many symbolic dishes. Bitter herbs are passed around to remind the family of the pain of bondage. Roast lamb is eaten to commemorate the offerings of the Israelites, and matzo bread commemorates the unleavened bread eaten by them on their journey.

The next festival in the Jewish year is Shavuot, which commemorates the giving of the laws to Moses. The Feast of the Tabernacles, Yom Kippur, and the Feast of Lots are also celebrated during the year.

SOVIET CELEBRATIONS

As part of the USSR, Belarus celebrated many official Soviet holidays with the other republics. Many of these festivals are still celebrated by Belarus and its neighbors to the east and west today. May Day and the October Revolution were two big celebrations in the Soviet Union, celebrated with massive displays of weapons and the products of industry. May Day is a traditional day for celebrating both the coming of spring and the rights of working people. The October Revolution marked the beginning of the Soviet way of life. This is no longer celebrated in Belarus. Instead, a much more popular public event is the celebration on July 27 of the brief period of independence in 1917.

MUSIC FESTIVALS

Belarus also took part in other festivals under the USSR, including various music festivals. During these, traditional music, opera, or classical music performers from all over the USSR would be brought together in one of the Soviet capitals. The USSR also had festivals celebrating Soviet art, literature, poetry, dance, and many other aspects of culture. Performances of music and displays of art from the other Soviet republics would be brought to Belarus as part of these festivals and friendly competitions would also take place.

In 1972 a poetry day was started. On this day, poets throughout Belarus would read their works. In 1974 a Minsk Festival of Music was organized and the festival continues to this day. Held in the last 10 days of November every year, the festival celebrates Belarusian music. It includes diverse performances from drum majorettes and traditional music and dancing. Many musicians perform in their traditional folk costumes.

Dancers in bridal dress perform at the Minsk Festival of Music.

FOOD

BELARUSIAN FOOD is quite unknown in the West. It is a home-style cuisine that uses ingredients available locally. Traditionally, a large clay stove was used for cooking. Although this type of stove is no longer in use, the style of dishes—slowly baked or stewed—has remained. As in other peasant cuisines, what is important is bulk rather than delicacy of taste. Belarusian dishes are based on the staples—bread, potatoes, cabbage, and pork, with mushrooms as an important ingredient in stuffings and sauces. Patties and pies are also very common.

Above: **There are now private markets selling fruit and vegetables such as this one in Grodno.**

Opposite: **A fruit vending stall in Minsk.**

In Soviet times the price of food was highly regulated and was only a small part of the family's budget. Public canteens in every town served workers cheap, wholesome food for lunch. The main family meal was in the evening. In modern times this situation has changed a great deal and people are experiencing price increases, food shortages, rationing, and long lines for food. Small plots of land and gardens at home have become very important, and in unofficial markets tiny amounts of vegetables and other foods change hands. The accident at Chernobyl has, of course, added to the problems of food shortage since large areas of cultivated land have now been abandoned. Livestock, wild animals that were once hunted for food, and the plant produce of the southern forests have become contaminated and now people have to guard against the danger of such food getting into the marketplace.

Fasting is an important part of the Eastern Orthodox religious cycle. At times of the year such as Lent, people have to give up meat and even dairy products. Right before Lent, therefore, all the fresh meat and dairy in the house is used up, and people start eating mostly vegetable dishes.

BREAD

One of the main food staples in Belarus is bread. White bread is popular in the cities and in the southern part of the country. One type of this bread is known as *kalachi* ("kal-AH-chi"), a small loaf made in the shape of a padlock. But the commonest form of bread is wholemeal rye bread. In the old days the dough would have been baked in the embers of the oven, then placed on cabbage or maple leaves, covered with a cloth to cool, and sprinkled with salt before eating.

Belarus has to import much of its wheat, partly due to the effects of Chernobyl and partly because the short wet summers in Belarus make wheat a difficult crop to grow. Since rye is a much easier crop and is widely grown in Belarus, rye bread is much more commonly eaten.

There have been many traditions associated with bread and its production in Belarus. Small pieces of the dough were given to children so that they could make their own small roll. Another traditional custom was to call the bread brought home from the day's farm work "hare's bread." If one dropped a piece of bread it was customary to pick it up and say "Lord forgive me!"

POTATOES

Potatoes are the main staple of the Belarusian diet and are grown through much of the country. There are a great many different ways of cooking potatoes in Belarus. The simplest method is to put them in the ashes of a fire until the potatoes are baked. After cooking they are sprinkled with salt and the flesh scooped out and eaten with butter or hemp oil.

There are also more elaborate ways of cooking potatoes. One method is to make dumplings from grated potatoes that are then stuffed with meat or mushrooms and baked in the oven. The dumplings are usually served as a side dish to meat.

Another common way of serving potatoes is to form them into pancakes called *dranniki* ("DRAN-ih-ki") and fry them with mushrooms and sour cream and often a side dish of pickled berries. Potato pies are also a popular way of cooking potatoes.

Above: **A busy market in Grodno. There can be long lines for food on some days.**

Opposite: **Presenting bread and salt is a traditional form of hospitality.**

117

Sausages are a popular Belarusian food.

MEAT DISHES

Pork is the most popular meat in traditional Belarusian cooking. Pig farming is carried out largely on factory farms, and pork is processed into bacon, ham, or sausages. A common pork dish is *kotleta pokrestyansky* ("kot-LET-ah polk-ress-tee-AN-skee")—pork cutlets served in mushroom sauce. Another dish popular in modern times and authentically Belarusian is *machanka* ("mah-CHAN-kah"), which is a thickened spicy gravy with pieces of pork served with pancakes. Beef steak is quite a luxurious meal and is popular too. The markets also offer wild game such as duck, pheasant, and geese; these are roasted or baked in earthenware pots and served with wild berry sauce. Lake and river fish such as perch, bream, loach, and crayfish are plentiful and are served at home and in restaurants. Fish roe is popular but can be very expensive.

Russian cooking is also quite common in a country where a large proportion of the population is ethnic Russian. Dishes such as chicken kiev and beef stroganoff feature on many hotel restaurant menus.

A RECIPE FOR STUFFED CUTLETS

$2^{1}/_{4}$ pounds (1 kg) boneless beef
salt and pepper
2 onions, finely chopped
$^{1}/_{4}$ pound (100 g) lard or butter
$^{1}/_{2}$ pound (225 g) breadcrumbs
    made from rye bread
$^{1}/_{4}$ pound (100 g) mushrooms,
    chopped

1 egg, beaten
$^{1}/_{2}$ teaspoon grated nutmeg
flour
2 cups beef stock
$^{1}/_{2}$ cup sour cream
mushroom soup (optional)

Slice the beef into thin slices. Pound it lightly with a meat tenderizer. Season beef slices with salt and pepper.

Fry the finely chopped onions in a little of the lard or butter. Remove from the heat and mix with the breadcrumbs. Add chopped mushrooms, beaten egg, and grated nutmeg, and season with salt and pepper to taste.

Spread some of the breadcrumb mixture on each of the beef cutlets and roll the cutlets into a tube, tying each with string. Sprinkle with flour.

Melt the remaining fat in a pan and add the rolled cutlets. Cover and cook over low heat until browned. Add beef stock and cover. Cook for 45 minutes. Add the sour cream and, if desired, some mushroom soup.

Transfer the cutlets to a plate, pour the stock over them and serve.

Samovars are Russian in origin but are still used to keep lots of hot tea readily available. They are large metal urns with a little tap to let the water out. However, in modern days many people are switching to kettles, and coffee is replacing tea as the popular drink.

KITCHENS

People in Belarus today have many modern appliances in their kitchens. Modern gas or electric stoves are used for most cooking, and refrigerators keep the food fresh. Canned and frozen foods can be bought at the supermarket. Many people eat out, especially at lunch time.

In the countryside, many modern houses are still built with a big cellar or an ice house in the yard. Ice houses have been used since the 15th century in Belarus. Known as *ledniks* ("LED-niks"), the ice houses are built of bricks and covered in earth. Often grass grows over them. They are used for cold storage of vegetables and preserves. Ice placed in them during winter may stay frozen well into the summer months.

The rich liked to serve some exotic delicacies at their banquets. Dishes such as elk lips served in sweetened vinegar or beaver's tails were not unusual.

A PEASANT'S DELIGHT

They brought on sauerkraut at first
Then soup with scratchings, piping hot.
Stiff millet-porridge then was served—
Make free with it and eat the lot!
Then jelly, and yogurt, nice and cool,
And gruel with pork fat swimming round,
And roasted geese, in a buttery pool,
Enough for all the gods was found.
And then they served fine sausages too,
And oatmeal pancakes by the score.
Taras wept tears of joy anew.

This is part of a 19th century poem, *Taras on Parnassus*, and describes some courses of a fine traditional meal. First is an appetizer, in this case, sauerkraut, a pickled cabbage often served cold in a kind of soup called *kapusta* ("kah-POOS-tah"). The next course would be a hot soup. There are many kinds to choose from. *Poliuka* ("POLL-yoo-kah") is hot soup thickened with flour. *Prantsak* ("pran-SAHK") is made from pearl barley and mushrooms. Other popular soups are made from potatoes seasoned with pork rinds, or combine noodles and chicken giblets. In spring, sorrel soup is popular as is nettle soup made from the common wayside plants. *Kvass* ("KVAHS") falls somewhere between a soup and a drink. As a soup, it is made from beetroot with meat, mushrooms, and vegetables added. A more common soup in modern Belarus is *borscht* ("BORSHT"), a plain beetroot soup that originated in the Ukraine and is served with sour cream. Jelly and yogurt would have been side dishes to enhance the taste of the food and clear the palate from one course to the next. The main course at this meal is goose, which would have been a rare part of a peasant meal since the birds were valuable and not often slaughtered.

Other cuisines are also becoming popular in Belarus. This is an Indian restaurant in Brest.

SWEETS AND DRINKS

Typical traditional sweet dishes in Belarus are pies made from local fruit such as apples or berries. Grapes are grown in the south as well as pears and strawberries. In modern Belarus, ice cream is popular and *Pinguin* is a popular chain of ice-cream parlors. Gingerbread and cakes made with honey are also common desserts.

The traditional drink of Belarus is birch juice. But more common nowadays is another drink called *kvass*—not to be confused with the soup of the same name. It is made from malt, flour, sugar, mint, and fruit. *Belovezhskaya* ("bel-ov-VYEH-skah-yah") is one of many popular herbal drinks and is believed to have a medicinal value. Cider, drinks made from honey, and locally brewed beer are also drunk, along with local versions of popular fizzy drinks. Tea is usually drunk black and coffee is becoming more popular. Alcohol is served in cafés and restaurants, but the law restricts the amount of vodka that can be served with food.

BELARUS

N

LATVIA

Lake Osveyskoye

RUSSIA

Western Dvina

Polotsk •

Polotsk Lowland

Vitebsk •

LITHUANIA

Lake Naroch

Orsha •

Vilnius •

Oshmyany Upland

B e l a r u s i a n   R i d g e

Dnieper

Mogilev •

▲ **MINSK**

Bykhov •

Dzerzhinska Mountain (1,135 ft / 346 m)

POLAND

Belovezhskaya Forest Nature Reserve

Grodno •

Neman

Svisloch

Neman Lowland

Bobruisk •

Slutsk •

Central Berezina Plain

Berezina

Dnieper

Soligorsk •

Gomel •

Berezina Nature Reserve

Pripet Nature Reserve

L o w l a n d

Pripet

Pripet

Pinsk •

Marshes

Bug

Dnieper

Brest •

Chernobyl •

UKRAINE

• Capital city
• Major town
▲ Mountain peak

Feet	Meters
16,500	5,000
9,900	3,000
6,600	2,000
3,300	1,000
1,650	500
660	200
0	0

Scale 1:3,400,000

0   25   50   75   100 Miles

0   50   100   150   200 Kilometers

QUICK NOTES

OFFICIAL NAME
Respublika Byelarus; Republic of Belarus

LAND AREA
80,200 square miles (207,700 square km)

CAPITAL
Minsk

POPULATION
10,494,000 (1994 estimate)

MAJOR TOWNS
Minsk, Pinsk, Grodno, Gomel, Vitebsk, Mogilev, Brest

HIGHEST POINT
Dzerzhinska Mountain (1,1,35 feet/346 m)

MAJOR RIVERS
Dnieper, Berezina, Pripet, Western Dvina, Neman

MAJOR LAKES
Lake Naroch, Lake Osveyskoye

LIFE EXPECTANCY
Men 66, women 75.7

INFANT MORTALITY
12.4 per 1,000 live births

CURRENCY
Belarusian ruble (5,854 rubli = US$1 in 1997)

PRINCIPAL LANGUAGES
Belarusian, Russian

MAJOR RELIGIONS
Christianity (Roman Catholic and Russian Orthodox), Judaism, Islam, atheism

MAJOR EXPORTS
machinery, chemicals, and petrochemicals

MAJOR IMPORTS
energy, raw materials, manufactured goods, wheat

LEADERS IN POLITICS
Stanislau Shushkevich, chairman of the Supreme Soviet 1991–94.
Alexander Lukashenko, president 1994–

IMPORTANT RELIGIOUS FESTIVALS
Easter: March/April
Orthodox Christmas: January 7
Catholic Christmas: December 25

OTHER HOLIDAYS
Independence Day: July 27
Remembrance Day: November 2
October Revolution Day: November 7
Labor Day: May 1

LEADERS IN LITERATURE
Vladimir Karatkevich, Yakub Kolas, Yanka Kupala, Simeon Polotski, Frances Skaryna, Anatol Sys

GLOSSARY

andraki ("and-RARK-ee")
Woolen winter skirts.

banya ("BAN-yah")
Bath house similar to a sauna.

dacha ("DAH-chah")
Country house.

icon
Miniature religious painting showing a scene from Christianity or a religious figure.

kalachi ("kal-AH-chi")
Small loaf of bread in the shape of a padlock.

karagods ("KAH-rah-gods")
Circles formed around bonfires by dancers.

kaski ("KAH-ski")
A moral tale.

Kryvici ("kree-VEE-chi")
Slavic tribe that lived in the Belarus region in the early centuries a.d.

Kupalle ("koo-PAH-leh")
Summer solstice festival in Belarus, with pagan origins.

kvass ("KVAHS")
Drink made from malt, flour, mint, and fruit.

lednik ("LED-nik")
Ice house to store vegetables and preserves.

perestroika ("per-es-TROY-ka")
The liberalizing of the USSR in the 1980s under Mikhail Gorbachev.

Polonization
The process of converting a country's culture to a Polish one.

rayoni ("ray-ON-ee")
Districts of Belarus (there are 141 of them).

Russification
The process of changing a country's language and culture to Russian culture.

Soviet
A name used to describe the style of government or cultural aspects of the Soviet Union. Also the name of the elected council in Belarus (although its continued existence is questionable).

Tatars
A group of Muslim people who first came to eastern Europe from the Middle East.

trasnyanka ("traz-YAN-kah")
A mixture of Russian and Belarusian spoken throughout Belarus.

UNESCO
United Nations Scientific and Cultural Organization.

voblasti ("VOH-blahst-EE")
Regional divisions.

BIBLIOGRAPHY

Belarus: Then & Now. Minneapolis: Lerner Geography Dept. Lerner Publications Co., 1993.

Coffey, Wayne. *Olga Korbut: Fearless Gymnast*. Olympic Gold. Woodbridge: Blackbirch Press, 1994.

Gosnell, Kelvin. *The Former Soviet States: Belarus, Ukraine, and Moldova*. London: Franklin Watts, 1992.

Harvey, Miles. *The Fall of the Soviet Union*. Cornerstone of Freedom. Danbury, CT: Children's Press, 1995.

Roberts, Elizabeth. *Focus on Russia and the Republics*. London: Evans Brothers, 1996.

INDEX

INDEX

INDEX